CW00666235

JUST THE TICKET

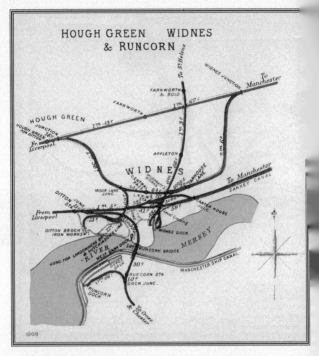

A Railway Clearing House map of the Widnes area. Farnworth on the CLC line became Widnes North, and the 'L&NW Sta' beneath 'Central Pass.' became Widnes South.

JUST THE TICKET

TICKET

Memories of a
Liverpool booking clerk, 1962-65

Barry Allen

A Silver Link Book

First published in 2019

British Library Cataloguing in Publication Data

A catalogue record for this book is available
from the British Library.

ISBN 978 1 85794 558 4

Silver Link Books
Mortons Media Group Limited
Media Centre
Morton Way
Horncastle
LN9 6JR

Tel/Fax: 01507 529529
email: sohara@mortons.co.uk
Website: www.nostalgiacollection.com

Printed and bound in the Czech Republic

AUTHOR'S NOTE

All author royalties from the sale of this book will go to charity,
namely the upkeep of a special railway carriage for the disabled.
    Please forgive me if certain details are incorrect, as I have
only my memory to rely on. With the passage of time it is
hard to recall things accurately, but I have stated events as I
remember them.

CONTENTS

FOREWORD
by Peter Kelly
Former editor of
Steam Railway,
Rail Enthusiast
and The Railway
Magazine

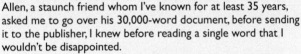

If you have thought that
being a humble booking
clerk with British Railways
was a dull and uninteresting
occupation, think again.

When Liverpool's Barry
Allen, a staunch friend whom I've known for at least 35 years,
asked me to go over his 30,000-word document, before sending
it to the publisher, I knew before reading a single word that I
wouldn't be disappointed.

Laced with Scouse humour from start to finish, it tells the
story of his three years in the job, starting at Widnes in 1962,
when he was just 16. Some of the stories will bring tears of
laughter to your eyes. Even the job selection process, which
entailed having a thorough medical and mental examination, had
me in stitches.

But there's also a serious side to Barry's book as he
laments the passing of the 'old ways' when the comforting
glow of coal fires, polished brass and hissing gas lamps gave an
atmosphere of warmth and continuity, and platform flower beds
surrounded by whitewashed stone borders reflected pride in
the job.

When he started work there were no fewer than three
stations in Widnes – North, South and Central – and on the
second day of his new job he managed to catch the train to

the wrong one! As a booking clerk's duties entailed helping passengers with timetables, this didn't go down too well with his superiors, but his chance to make amends by catching a string of a new type of highly explosive detonator thrown from the cab of an accelerating Stanier tank had me rolling with laughter.

On another occasion a porter told the wide-eyed teenager that, whenever a station inspection took place, each piece of coal in the scoops beside the fires would have to be hand polished by the trainee.

Once Barry had to weigh a large biscuit tin addressed to Sheffield and labelled 'Live Bait' – but when the string broke after weighing, all hell was let loose as a heaving mass of live maggots dropped on the floor.

Then there was a time when someone planted a dead mouse in a colleague's lunch box!

In an unstoppable stream, the stories just keep coming, and as he reels off the memories Barry's writing style makes you think you're right there beside him, and his description of the many gritty characters he came across are so vivid, you can almost see and feel them.

I heartily recommend this book, which opens a warm and colourful window on a long -vanished world and covers everything from the 'Big Freeze' of 1962-63 to notorious football specials, a lady passenger's insistence on carrying a small dog in a bag to avoid buying a proper ticket for her canine companion, and a railwayman's recollection of a river of rats running through Liverpool during the wartime blitz on the city.

In fact, if I were a TV producer I'd be reading it from cover to cover, for it contains everything I'd need to launch one of the funniest comedy series of all time. Thanks to Barry's vivid imagination and pinpoint powers of recollection, the stories are there in profusion, so all I'd have to find would be the right characters and the right preserved railway to base it around.

So read on and enjoy, for it's a story that has to be told and one for which we've been waiting for a very long time!

FOREWORD
by
Chris Eldon Lee
Retired writer,
broadcaster and radio
producer, formerly with
BBC Radio 4 and others

I first met Barry over a microphone
30 years ago. He'd been booked onto my show to talk about
his new volume of railway poems. Between the verses, Barry
talked about his passion for steam and his love of railways. The
depth of his memory and the clarity of his recollections clearly
struck a chord with my audience, who demanded more. So he
returned to my BBC Radio Merseyside studio again and again
and became a popular contributor.

Meeting over a pint one night, even more memories came
tumbling out. I simply said to him, 'You know, you ought to
write all this down.'

'You're right,' he replied. 'I should get it down on paper.'

It took Barry a while to come up with his first volume of
prose, *School Days and Steam Days*, which was ostensibly fiction,
but based largely on his own childhood in the 1950s and '60s.
He proudly sent me a copy. I read it from cover to cover and
really enjoyed it.

But it wasn't quite the story I had in mind. Barry had
actually worked on the railway in a period of great change,
when the old ways gave way to the new. That was what I really
wanted to read about.

Now the book, brimming with humour, is in your hands and
it's been well worth waiting for.

Buy it, soak up the steam, and relive some magical moments
from the golden era of British Railways.

INTRODUCTION

On browsing through the Social History section of my local
library, I was amazed to find just how many railway books now
feature personal reminiscences. Various subjects from footplate
experiences to signalling recollections perched beseechingly
on an endless shelf, and I wondered if there was room for
another. Common sense screamed the answer; however, sound
thinking often succumbs to human emotion. I noticed that none
featured experiences written by a booking clerk, an occupation
most people think dull and uninteresting. Since my own
exploits in this job could hardly be described as dull, I decided
to put pen to paper and reflect on my own career in this said
profession.

Humour forms the basis of my story, without which
life would be much the poorer. I should add that all events
mentioned are based of fact, and most individuals mentioned
are now retired or sadly deceased.

My career with British Railways was extremely short, a
mere three years. My service commenced during the twilight
of steam, a period best known to railwaymen as pre-Beeching,
when Britain still had a large railway system, and perhaps a
happy one! Modernisation was on the march, but BR still
managed to convey cattle, horses and pigeons. Steam, like the
whale, fought for survival, clinging wearily to its now precarious
throne. Not infrequently would I witness a diesel or electric
locomotive's demise, steam deputising with apparent relish,
the drivers sometimes achieving the impossible with their run-
down chargers. These stories are best told by others, and I have
no wish to enlarge upon this theme.

Electrification, still the order of the day, spread slowly
northwards, erasing the old stations with gay precision. Gone
forever the glowing coal fires, polished brasswork and hissing
gas lamps, and with them went the atmosphere of warmth and

The booking clerk

Punch, punch, punch goes the man behind the glass
Handing out three returns to the couple with their lass. The
money's now flying, loud the chink of change;
The passengers now move on, the queue it's rearranged.
Punch, punch, punch goes the man who is seldom seen,
Issuing three green singles, change at Aberdeen.
Two returns for London, but they want to take their dog;
The man looks up with sullen face, his mind is still agog.
Swift concentration, a burst upon his pen,
Hasty calculations, now he's ready again.
Punch, punch, punch goes the man you can never hear.
How much for Glasgow?
My gosh, it seems so dear!
Two mid-weeks for Liverpool, a Mercantile for Crewe,
A Forces return for Inverness, my God what a to-do!
Punch, punch, punch goes the man who's working hard;
A privilege return for Newcastle, the customer's a guard.
The pace seems to quicken, the queue is getting long;
The customers are always right, try telling them they're wrong!
The strain's now increasing, the pressure begins to tell –
Here is a cheeky boy, to the clerk he's giving hell.
Suddenly the clerk appears standing by the boy,
He's not looking happy, his face contains no joy.
Punch, punch, punch goes the man behind the glass.

Barry Allen

welcome. The latter vanished unseen, never to be replaced by any modern structure.

It was into this changing world that I stepped, with the self assurance and naivety of a schoolboy, who, after spending his life trainspotting on busy station platforms, thought he knew all about railways and the people who ran them. Surprisingly I learned that not all engine drivers stood next to God, and for the man on the dole the railway was often the last resort, with its poor pay and unsociable hours.

Although my story concerns events relating to the North West, a lot of my experiences were undoubtedly acted out by other individuals, in stations the length and breathe of the UK. I never wanted to become a booking clerk, but fate, that irrepressible force, decreed otherwise. To a steam-mad 16-year-old, a booking clerk was indeed a most boring occupation, and certainly one to be avoided at all costs....

I
A CAREER BEGINS

During the summer of 1961 the decision was made by my parents to keep me at school an extra year, as I had done well the previous term. This would give me a chance to take additional examinations, which, if passed, greatly increased my job prospects. Quite a few of my fellow school pals also received this opportunity, including Philip Ebsworth who, like myself, had a railway career in mind. Railway work had its drawbacks, due to the low rates of pay, but after spending endless hours trainspotting on station platforms I felt that railways were in my blood. Frequent conversations with my Uncle Jim further convinced me that this was the career for me, and heaven help anyone who thought otherwise. My uncle, who was employed as a BR signalman, used to reiterate that there were some good jobs to be had on the railway. Now all I had to do was to get one.

Philip and I both applied for employment with British Railways, then administered by the British Transport Commission, in the early months of 1962, an action that led to an interview at Lime Street Chambers with Mr J. Pye. At this interview he asked me questions about my hopes and aspirations, detailing the types of employment available and stating that any future employment was subject to the applicant passing the necessary medical and educational examinations. I came away feeling fairly confident, thinking that if I passed the exams there would be a place for me in Traffic Control, a department that my uncle had informed me was one of the most interesting and arduous.

Finally the day came to take the Railway Board's educational examination, and by chance Philip would be accompanying me. On entering Lime Street Chambers, we were greeted by a small queue outside the examination room and our hearts fell.

Invitation to an interview,
26 March 1962.

Invitation to a clerical
examination.

After exchanging nervous glances, we entered, each wishing each other well as we took our seats for the pending tests. The examinations, as I recall, were fairly tough, especially the mental arithmetic test, which took me by surprise; however, I soldiered on and completed all the papers placed before me. Once the exams were over, the examiner uttered that classic phrase, 'We will be in touch.' I left feeling rather apprehensive, although my spirits arose with every step that took me away from that dreaded room. Words were exchanged as to how we had fared; however, the best policy was to wait and see, a reaction that saw me greet every postal delivery during the coming days. A week went by and the expected letter arrived. Watched by my mother, I opened it and to my great joy – need I say more – the last paragraph stated that I would be required to take a medical at Liverpool Central station.

On one of the hottest days of the year I found myself knocking on the door of the medical office, having been to the toilet a couple of times, such was my nervousness. On entering

I found myself in front of a middle-aged gentleman who, after asking my name, wanted to know if I had had a number of disorders, which included everything from yellow fever to the dreaded 'clap'. Seemingly disappointed at my negative replies, he proceeded to check me for colour blindness. This involved picking numbers from a book containing a sea of colours. Then came a physical examination, followed by a request for a sample of my water. Unfortunately this I could not do, so, after handing me a beaker, he suggested that I go to the station cafeteria and have a cup of tea, returning when he felt that I could carry out his request.

This I duly did, but instead of having one cup, I had two, as I was hot and nervous. On my return I was swiftly handed the beaker and told to perform my duty. Once I had started I could not stop! A seemingly comical situation developed as the doctor shouted, 'Whoa, whoa, whoa,' while I was thinking, 'No, no, no.' A small pool appeared and, to my intense relief, I eventually stopped. Still, he had a sample of my water – and so did every other person using the station, was my unspoken thought. With a sense of relief, I left the room, hopefully never to return, such was my embarrassment, with the usual 'We'll be in touch' ringing in my ears.

Approximately a week after my medical, I received a letter stating that all was well and instructing me to report for work a week after I had left school. This meant that I would not have a summer holiday. I was not unduly bothered, as I was keen to start; however, the days dragged on until finally my school life was at an end. I said goodbye with mixed feeling. Good friends are hard to find, and the fact that so many people would be going out of my life forever was a sobering thought.

The following Monday I reported to Mr Pye at Lime Street

The free ticket issued to me for my interview.

Chambers. He informed me that I was to become a trainee booking clerk at Widnes North station on the old Cheshire Lines Committee (CLC) system. On arrival I was to report to the Station Master, Mr Derek Halstead. This news came as a great blow, the vision of a job in Traffic Control rapid disappearing. Mr Pye went on to say that we couldn't all be

Station Master Derek Halstead is seen here during a rail strike in the 1960s. Note the former waiting room and booking office on the Manchester platform. *8D Association*

Traffic Controllers, but if I was successful in my new job there was nothing to stop me applying for that department at a later date. I left his office clutching a railway ticket for my journey, together with a free pass, allowing me to travel from Garston station to Widnes North. I could not hide my disappointment as I walked to Liverpool Central, my hopes seemingly shattered. Still, all was not lost, and by the time I boarded the diesel railcar my spirits had risen somewhat.

Widnes boasted three stations. Widnes South served the former LNWR route, providing a limited service to the local area, and closed during my stay at Widnes North. All expresses to Manchester Central stopped at both Widnes North and

WIDNES NORTH
TRAIN DEPARTURES

BRITISH RAILWAYS

18th JUNE to 9th SEPTEMBER 1962

WEEKDAYS

SUNDAYS

The Summer 1962 timetable at Widnes North.

Warrington Central, providing an excellent train service between the main cities. The third station was Widnes Central, which this was located in the centre of Widnes, just like it says on the tin. It was served by a loop line departing from the Cheshire Lines system at Hough Green station, and had only a limited service. In the past it had provided, together with Tanhouse Lane, a good service for people using the adjacent factories, but by the 1960s had fallen from grace. This station was also to close within a few years, leaving only Widnes North serving the town.

My journey was uneventful until I reached Widnes North. After alighting, I anxiously sought out a member of staff, only to find Bart Purcell, one of the porters. Swiftly I introduced myself; we then walked to the booking office, where I was to meet the boss. During our walk he asked me if I was interested in horses, shaking his head at my negative reply. He informed me that if I ever wanted any advice on the subject, he was the man to see. If it was sex, then I should see Clifford, as he was undoubtedly an expert, and knew all the answers.

At Widnes North in the early 1960s are Derek Halstead and his wife (left), Bart (centre) and, I think, Mrs Boyd and her husband John.
Courtesy of the Widnes 8D Association

On reaching the booking office we met John Boyd, one of the booking clerks. He informed me that I was a bloody fool for joining the railway, as there was no money in it, and recommended that I join the Ford Motor Company instead. This was a sentiment he later endorsed, as he left a few months later to join that concern.

Gingerly I entered the booking office, Bart's whispering not helping my concentration. At least I knew where to go to find the *Men Only* magazine, and the promise of a cup of tea in the porters' office seemed most tempting. Even though the sunlight pierced the open door, the office seemed dark and forbidding. Derek Halstead stood by a hissing gas lamp, and behind him sat Bill Kirk, seemingly glued to an old-fashioned high stool. The Station Master welcomed me and asked about my hopes and aspirations, while Bill looked on. Then Bill began to rock on his stool as he methodically puffed his pipe, his piercing gaze like that of a headmaster confronting a naughty child.

Oh, so I had wanted to become an engine driver? He had found a weakness for possible future exploitation. His piped smoked heavily, and the 'blower' was clearly on, as he added that most drivers were rogues, and the less I had to do with them the better. This stemmed from the fact that Bill was employed as a Grade 3 clerk on pensions and pay bills, and he had fought the Germans and engine drivers with equal ferocity. The Station Master then asked if I would like a cup of tea, somewhat relieving an unhappy recruit. Swiftly he handed me the kettle, explaining that I had just volunteered for my first duty, adding that it should be just up my street, as I could watch the steam come from the kettle! Thus I received my first duty, and heaven help the trainee who forgot the kettle – I quickly learned a new and fruity vocabulary.

Like a puppy exploring its new home, I took the opportunity to acquaint myself with my new workplace. Every nook and cranny was inspected with relish. To my surprise the coal place contained only coal, which Bart insisted had to be polished by the trainee when there was a station inspection! Later in the day the Station Master suggested that I should try my hand at collecting tickets. I departed to my allotted task full of enthusiasm, and Bart's presence gave me renewed confidence. An express from Manchester rolled in, and I was suddenly confronted by a group of rushing platelayers. To my utter amazement, on requesting their passes I was trust aside and told to 'get stuffed', or words to that effect, as the members of the travelling public dutifully put their tickets in my outstretched palm. By now all confidence had evaporated and the last passenger showed me his pass with a sympathetic smile. I walked to the booking office completely shattered, and handed over the collected tickets to Bart. I had just learned a harsh lesson. Nothing is as easy as it looks and that there is no substitute for experience. Ticket collecting would become second nature during the coming months, but on my first day it proved an unhappy reminder of the impetuosity of youth.

The station gardens were Derek Halstead's pride and joy – information gleaned from Signalman Danny Briscoe. Working with his brother in Widnes North box, he was also a keen gardener. The colourful display surrounding his garden, alongside Derek's efforts on the station bank, presented the public with a wonderful display. Antirrhinums and mesembryanthemums, together with other annuals, blazed in the sunlight, each bed surrounded by white painted stones, reflecting the pride that still prevailed on the former Cheshire Lines system.

It is difficult to describe the events of my first day; I probably achieved and learned little, as all statements and explanations were received in a flurry of enthusiasm and excitement. Still, it was tired teenager who boarded the railcar for home. I had so much to tell my parents, and could not wait to get home. Little did I know that the next day would prove an embarrassing ordeal for a naive young booking clerk, and one that I was not likely to forget for a very long time.

2
I DROP SOME CLANGERS

The following day I arose early, allowing myself plenty of time to catch the 7.58am Garston to Manchester stopping train. After catching a bus to Garston, I found myself alone in the station's bay platform. In it stood No 43045, an Ivatt Class 4 tender engine that was heading my Manchester train. I was overjoyed at the thought of being pulled by a steam engine. After checking with the guard if the train stopped at Widnes, I boarded, taking my place in a former non-corridor suburban carriage, built to handle the bulk of the busy commuter traffic. As with steam, these carriages were in decline and I quickly settled down to what was to prove to be an eventful journey.

All went well until we reached Hough Green station. On

A Fowler 2-6-4 tank speeds through Garston station on the former CLC with a Manchester train. This was my departure point for Widnes North, and I spent a lot of time in the signal box as a lad. Alas, this station is no more. *R. Stephens*

departure the engine suddenly swung onto the loop line for
Widnes Central, and I immediately realised that I had caught
the wrong train! I could imagine my embarrassment when I
had to explain my late arrival at Widnes North, and I began to
feel very worried indeed! Quickly Widnes Central arrived and
I immediately informed Ann, one of the two lady porters, of my
dilemma. Rather amused, she telephoned Mr Halstead to inform
him of my problem, while I caught a bus to the correct station.
After alighting, I gathered myself for the ensuing fray. Intrepidly
I entered the booking office, amid peals of laughter and witty
remarks. Already it was common knowledge down the line,
and as one wag later put it, I'd never make a railwayman as long
as I had a hole in my arse! Another bright spark sent me an
application form for a free bus pass. My career was off to an
inauspicious start.

Once things had calmed down a little, the Station Master
gave me a ticking off for my mistake. The public often requested

At Widnes Central in 1964 porter (or is it porteress?) Ann O'Lohan
wheels a barrow containing a vast amount of parcels along the
platform. *Courtesy of the Widnes 8D Association*

timetable information, and it was hardly going to inspire confidence if I couldn't read basic timetable information. I could make amends, however; a light engine would shortly be arriving with some detonators for the signal box. I was instructed to collect the detonators from the driver, but on no account was I to drop them, as they were a new type and highly explosive.

Tensely I waited for the engine and within minutes a Stanier tank appeared puffing towards me at a very slow pace. On reaching the platform end, the driver opened the regulator, rapidly increasing speed, while the young fireman leered out of the cab clutching a string of detonators attached to a piece of wire. As the engine sped past the fireman threw the detonators in the air, shouting, 'For Christ sake, don't drop them!', then he and the driver leaned out of the cab to watch the ensuing fun. I remember catching the rapidly descending package, only to feel it slipping through my sweating palms and fall with a bang on the platform. I probably went several shades of white during those fateful seconds, and was awoken from my stupor by a chorus of laughter. I turned to find the entire station staff, including the Station Master, peering around the office door, each in a state of mirth. The joke had been planned in typical railway fashion. My last recollection of the incident was a vee sign from the fireman, as the engine, continuously blowing its whistle, sped off leaving in its wake a distraught clerk and a handful of comedians. I must confess that I soon saw the funny side of the prank, but equally I was determined to gain my revenge as quickly as possible.

I spent a lot of time with Clifford, one of the booking clerks, who was something of a lad when it came to young ladies. He would chat them up in the waiting room, much to Dick's disapproval. Clifford was extremely handsome, so he seldom failed in his task.

As the main waiting room lay just outside the booking office, Dick would wait until Clifford had seemingly made a conquest, then shout to him that his wife and kids were on the phone. Clifford's comments are unprintable, but he soon got wise to Dick, and switched his activities to the up platform, where he was out of Dick's sight. Clifford often explained that he was just a good 'PR man' for British Railways, and a youngster like me could learn a lot by watching an expert! To Dick, Clifford was just a bloody sex maniac, but Bart thought differently, and could be often found listening to Clifford's stories.

Widnes was not far from the USAF base at Burtonwood, and the appearance one morning of a USAF Major in the parcels section of the main booking office caused more than a ripple of interest.

'Excuse me, sir,' he said, gazing in my direction, while I fidgeted around.

'Who me?' I exclaimed, jumping off my stool.

'Yes, sir.' Sixteen and a 'sir' – I was flabbergasted. 'Could I have a word with you?'

I walked over, watched intensely by Bill and the Station Master. The Major quickly explained that he would be sending his son to school the following morning, and requested that I keep an eye on his offspring; after all, he did not want him to catch the wrong train. This brought chuckles from Bill, who had been studying the officer's decorations. As if on cue, the Major's son appeared, and we were introduced. When Bill later enquired as to where his father had obtained all his medals, his lad immediately replied, 'Fighting the Sioux.'

At Derek's request I enrolled for the forthcoming night school classes run by British Railways on 'Booking office and parcel procedures'. I should learn my trade, enthused the Station Master, and on my first outing I found myself standing in a small queue outside the old goods office in Great Howard Street, a building long since demolished. This haven proved unsuitable, and within a few weeks we had switched to a room in Liverpool Central. The new venue provided an excellent view of the busy station, and I immediately sat at the rear to watch all the traffic, especially the steam-hauled stock. With the general heat and people smoking, it was hard to concentrate on what was to all and sundry a thoroughly boring subject. A steam locomotive blowing off drowned out the instructor completely.

On many occasions I witnessed an apparently silent tutor, trying valiantly to break through a stupor of indifference. I recall him asking a pupil to state how he would send a basket of pigeons to Guernsey. 'Release them and let them fly there,' whispered a nearby joker, doing his crossword. I must confess that these classes are best forgotten, and apart from the small interlude mentioned I have no great memory of the course.

The station management regularly held station inspections and it just so happened that we were subject to such a check at the beginning of August. The gardens received additional attention, as well as the station. Mr Halstead was keen to do well, hoping no doubt to win the garden prize, or a commendation. Nervously we awaited our visitors, who arrived behind a Stanier Class 4 tank engine, hauling a gleaming inspection saloon; the latter contrasted sharply with the train engine, which had not been picked for its external condition. Bart was quick to point out that the coach was stocked with food and drink, demonstrating the status of the entourage. Unfortunately the weather had become rather overcast, hence the failure of the Station Master's prize blooms to open. Any reader with gardening knowledge will know that mesembryanthemums only open in full sunlight, therefore the gardens were not at their best. Alas, all Derek's efforts seemed to have been in vain; however, he did receive the comment, 'Keep up the good work.' Bart later remarked that the comment had reminded him of his captain during the war, although he must have been in his short trousers! I think I am right in saying that complete inspection took no longer than 10 minutes, during which time I was introduced to Mr Byrom, the Passenger Manager. He shook my hand vigorously.

'Nice to see you again' he enthused. Since we had never met, his remark left me perplexed. and it was clearly a case of mistaken identity. Mr Cochrane, the Traffic Manager, having satisfied himself as to the condition of the Gents, called a halt to proceedings and they left for Sankey. Later we were pleased to hear that Mr Halstead had won the garden prize and the inspection had proved satisfactory.

In the early 1960s Widnes North Station Master Derek Halstead
receives a commendation, or possibly a garden prize, from Mr
Cochrane. On the left is Bart Purcell, and on the right Tommy Connor.
Courtesy of the Widnes 8D Association

One could seldom relax during a period of duty, as it was
an extremely busy station, and no more so than on Thursday
afternoons, when it was half-day closing. Then we would
be swamped with passengers for the Southport excursion,
standing room only being the order of the day. Mr Halstead
ran a tight ship, tolerating no slackness and making sure that
his staff carried out their duties correctly and courteously, no
matter what the pressure. Fortunately he was blessed with a
keen sense of humour and had a lively personality. I recall one
occasion when he instructed a booking clerk to return home
and change from his jeans into a pair of trousers. His request
did not go down well with certain staff members, but the
employee complied, respecting the Station Master's wishes. One
could not imagine a similar situation arising today. A lot of pride
vanished with modernisation. Such is progress, or the lack of it!

We had two booking offices, unlike other stations. The main booking office was on the westbound platform, with the other smaller structure on the eastbound, serving Manchester. Due to the volume of traffic, it was necessary to employ two booking clerks on days, while a third operated on the twilight shift, often popular, as it offered a respite from the daily bustle. Booking clerks John Boyd, Jimmy Tate and Joe Ushin, Clifford's replacement, covered the three turns in rotation. Trainees were normally allocated to the day shift to gain experience. The station had two porters, Tommy Connor and Bart Purcell, who covered both early and late turns. Tommy was in his late 50s, but was in many ways as lively as Bart. One had to be on guard when working with either, mischief being second nature to a British Railways porter.

The porter

'Will you carry my bags? Oh, the pushchair as well?
Here, take hold of our Tommy and grab our Michelle.'
A grunting reply, then he bends to his task.
Funny the chores a porter is asked:
'What time's my connection, if I'm changing at Crewe?'
'Was my wife on the local that's just been through?'
A utility man with a bag full of tricks,
From putting up posters to trimming lamp wicks,
Issuing tickets, parcels and such,
Carry suitcases – 'Oh thanks very much.'
Given the chance he'll be off to the pub
Or fitfully doze by the fire so snug.
But he's a resilient chap in cold, wet or shine,
A bubbling comedian, he's known down the line.
Polishing, carting, all part of his chores,
Brushing, weeding, shutting train doors.
Shift work, lift work, no easy touch:
'Carry your bag, sir?' 'Oh thanks very much!'
Barry Allen

My duties encompassed a large variety of tasks, including the collecting and issuing of tickets, balancing cash and books, dealing with timetables enquiries, and the dispatching and receiving of parcels. It was this latter chore that led to a rather amusing incident concerning myself and a tin of live white maggots.

A rather aged gentleman presented himself at the counter with a large square biscuit tin labelled 'LIVE BAIT'. He wanted to send it to Sheffield, but on inspecting the tin I noticed that it was poorly tied, the string being somewhat frayed. Enquiring as to its safety, I received the reply that it had been carried uneventfully for over half a mile, so it was reasonable to assume that it was safe. Still a little dubious, I picked the tin up by the string, moving it up and down, and, once satisfied, placed it on the scales. After weighing, I again lifted the tin, when suddenly the string snapped and the lid flew off, discharging the contents all over the office floor. My cursing and shouting soon attracted the attention of my colleagues, who on inspecting the wriggling mass thought it highly amusing. Their advice was to brush the maggots up before they wriggled up my trousers – advice I promptly took. Aided by the aged customer, who was by now apologising profusely, I swept the maggots onto a shovel, and managed to clear up the mess. Bart magically appeared once we had refilled the tin, and offered me the loan of his fishing rod, which led to the exchange of some choice remarks. But one thing bothered me – the tin did not appear to be full, and I began to wonder how much it had originally held. Still, there was nothing I could do, so it was retied and reweighed and placed outside. I was more than grateful when the customer departed, still apologising.

This was not the end of the episode, however, as we constantly came across maggots in various places in the office. This tended to put us off eating our lunch, as seeing a maggot in your sandwich box can be quite disconcerting, and one wondered how it had got there! Later we seemed to have a fair number of bluebottles, but this was just a coincidence – at least, that was my story.

I have previously mention Joe Ushin, who had joined us with the closure of Widnes South; he was Clifford's replacement, who had left to find fame and fortune elsewhere. Joe loved an unknown group called the Beatles, and suggested I visit the Cavern Club in Liverpool to see them. He was convinced that one day they would be superstars, but at this point we would disagree. I mean, their name was ridiculous, and would have to be changed. (Any reader can guess why I never became a success.) Joe soon settled in and I quickly found his strengths and weaknesses, to be exploited at the earliest opportunity, just as he no doubt discovered mine!

Working with Jimmy Tate proved to be a real joy. Of Irish extraction, he would enthral me with tales of his youth in Ireland. He was both humorous and intelligent, having gained school teaching qualifications before finishing up as a booking clerk for British Railways. If Jimmy had a weakness, is was giving out timetable information, as he sometimes got mixed up with his am's and pm's (thankfully we now have the 24-hour clock thus eliminating the confusion created by the former system). This could be a problem, especially when reading the various regional timetables, some more complex than others. One Saturday morning an extremely elderly couple entered the office to enquire about the trains from Widnes North to Shrewsbury. Jimmy decided to deal with their enquiry and I was instructed to watch and gain experience.

The couple were, to use a well-known expression, like 'Darby and Joan' and came armed with pen and paper. When Jimmy asked which way they preferred to go, they replied, 'By train.' We glanced at each other, knowing that this was going to take some time! Jimmy then went on to explain that they could travel by two routes, either from Liverpool Lime Street, via Crewe, or Birkenhead Woodside, via Chester. They both agree to go via Crewe, but insisted that they preferred to travel from Widnes North to Crewe, which was not possible. Finally he persuaded them to travel from Runcorn, much to his relief. Then he proceeded to quote the necessary train times, which were swiftly written down by the elderly gentleman; however, no sooner had Jimmy made a statement than it was retracted, as he was having trouble with his am's and pm's. The gentleman kept writing away and after a few minutes had compiled a completely useless list. I was now near to hysterics, and Jimmy was receiving a frosty look from the Station Master.

To add to Jimmy's problems, the gentleman suddenly insisted that there was a train that use to run to Shrewsbury as he remembered it running after the First World War. This was too much for me, so I left to visit the toilet, as I was having trouble controlling myself. On returning I found the gentleman telling his wife that perhaps they might be better travelling by bus, which nearly caused Jimmy to blow a fuse. I was loving every minute when the Station Master intervened and instructed Jimmy to attend to the booking office window. I was to take over, which meant that I had to convince the couple that the train he mentioned no longer ran and the railways had been nationalised in 1948, bringing grunts of disapproval.

Thus I earned my pay, and small incidents such as this kept me going, especially when I felt frustrated and angry because a passenger had just ranted at me about a late arrival or similar. I was glad of these intervals for light relief, and looked forward eagerly to the next.

3
OF MICE AND MEN

Now I know that operating staff liked a pint, and it was not unusual for drivers, firemen and guards to enjoy a couple of pints before signing on and off. They were probably so experienced at this practice that it did not cause problems. There were many railway clubs associated with areas or sheds, and it generally worked well for all concerned. Alcohol taken in excess, however, can cause serious problems.

The sight of the Harwich express heading to Manchester proved an irresistible lure, therefore I would, opportunity permitting, manage to be on the platform before its arrival. Steam-hauled, it would thunder through at approximately 75mph, creating a mini whirlwind. One clear and sunny afternoon I watched the train's rapid approach when a sudden blast from the Station Master's whistle signified impending danger. Turning, I saw one of the porters nonchalantly standing in the train's path, clumsily trying to retrieve a parcel from the eastbound platform. Again Mr Halstead blew his whistle, frantically shouting instructions to the inebriated porter, but to no avail. Shrilly the express's whistle broke the air, while I watched in frozen horror. More frantic whistle blowing from the Station Master and engine crew at last produced the necessary effect, and the culprit moved hesitantly away from the up line on to the down. The express thundered through, its driver briefly displaying his anger with a piercing stare.

Mr Halstead, also livid, led the offender to his office, tersely informing me to carry on with my duties. I was later informed that the guilty party had been sent home as he was feeling unwell. This was said no doubt for my benefit, but I suspect that the Station Master had no option but to suspend the porter on the spot. Not a pleasant task, but necessary, for an intoxicated man on duty is a menace to himself and his workmates, and can provide them with quite a fright.

Bart popped into the office one afternoon with a real gem. One of the booking clerks, who shall remain nameless, did not like mice. The word was out, and the booking clerk was soon to regret his passing remark. Now, it so happened that the booking office was one of their favourite haunts, so traps were set by the Station Master and checked each morning. The clerk in question was due to book a race special to Haydock Park, so we decided to play a joke on him. As we entered the eastbound booking office, Bart had a dead mouse in his possession, and we placed the dead creature behind the dating press, where we thought it would be swiftly seen.

Race specials were generally popular, and the period before their arrival was usually hectic. Many of the punters were mingling with the professional bookies, hoping to pick up a juicy tip. Bart was doing likewise, as backing horses was his great love, and he was not going to let such an opportunity pass. Tips were normally picked up with ease, the horse's name being whispered in the punter's ear, after the solemn promise that they would keep the information to themselves. Having given such an assurance, they would immediately tell all their mates waiting on the platform. Later on, hearing the results, we often found out that the horses were unplaced, and assumed that the professional bookies had passed false information to increase the odds.

The clerk had by now entered the booking office, so I followed in his wake, positioning myself to his rear as he opened the hatch. It was difficult to keep a straight face on seeing the little dead mouse peeping out at him. Soon he was working flat out, continually punching tickets and giving out change. In fact, he was working so swiftly that he had not noticed the mouse. After a few minutes Bart reappeared for an update on events. I was just about to express my disappointment when a sharp cry rang out and the clerk came flying out of the booking office like a bat out of hell. Bart and I were in raptures, tears trickling down our faces, such was our delight. The clerk, who had now guessed the source of the prank, was clearly not amused, uttering some unrepeatable oaths. When we were sufficiently recovered, I noticed that a rather alarming queue had developed outside the unmanned booking office. Pointing to the restless punters, I suggested to the clerk that it might be prudent to resume his duties, but he flatly refused.

By now I was becoming apprehensive and, fearing the appearance of the Station Master, I entered the booking office, receiving a certain amount of abuse from the waiting passengers. The train had been sighted, and for the next few minutes I worked like a mad man. I swear the mouse was smiling at me, and even if it wasn't the clerk certainly was. The joke had truly backfired, and the clerk was getting great satisfaction from seeing me doing his job. I was more than happy when the last punter received his ticket, by which time the train was standing in the platform behind my old friend Ivatt Class 4 No 43045.

On reflection, this prank still reigns supreme, and the thought of it makes me smile more than 50 years later. The memory of the clerk's face as he fled the office is still implanted in my mind. A couple of years later the Haydock Park branch passed into oblivion, and one cannot help wondering how it would have fared today. Immensely popular, its demise was probably short-sighted, and politics played a big part in many line closures.

Now the recipient of our little joke soon got his own back, and I was to become his victim. A couple of days later he informed me in a serious manner that a lady had got stuck in the toilet, the door having jammed due to the damp. He was going to get the Station Master, but in the meantime I was to try to open the door from the outside. Like a fool, I believed him and entered the ladies toilet to find the door closed. Shouting to the occupant to keep back, I kicked the door, only to hear an almighty shriek. The penny immediately dropped, and I left in some haste, making for the safety of the booking office. On arrival I found the door locked, and a leering face pressed against the window. The clerk was having fun. Turning, I was confronted by an agitated old lady, who demanded to see the Station Master. Had I seen anyone leaving the toilet, she enquired. Thinking quickly, I said that I had seen someone emerge and that they had left by the nearest exit. I then added that it was the Station Master's day off and I would report it to him the following morning. Heaven knows what colour my face was, and I was secretly cursing the clerk throughout my conversation with the unfortunate victim. The old lady seemed satisfied with my explanation, and went on her way. I was now on my guard, and would never make the same mistake again.

I wonder how many readers remember the 'Cuban Missile Crisis'. This historic confrontation between East and West proved a tense period for most of us. Joe especially was quite convinced that Armageddon lay just days away. He would read each newspaper report with growing pessimism and this tended to have a knock-on effect. Most of the staff more than breathed a sigh of relief once this episode had passed. Bart used to quip that the whole crisis could have been avoided had the Russians shipped their missiles by British Railways; then they would have been lost in transit and the crisis would have been over! We were not amused.

Welcome visitors were police patrolmen, who sometimes popped in for quick cup of tea and a visit to the toilet, or vice versa, all in the line of duty. To say that they could tell a tale was an understatement. I would listen enthralled to their amusing stories and endless frustrations. On late turn they would be especially welcome. You could feel vulnerable on such a lonely shift and an encounter with a drunk or abusive individual was not uncommon. If our visitors were unlucky, they might arrive just in time for one of Jimmy Tate's brews. Sometimes this consisted of not emptying the teapot prior to adding fresh tea, giving it a wonderful texture. The policemen would politely refuse one of his brews, suddenly remembering that they something to do and disappearing. The rest of us would either dredge the tea leaves from the cup, or pour the drink down the sink when his back was turned. As for Jimmy, he would drink it without so much as a grimace.

Nearly all the Cheshire Lines stations incorporated a Station Master's house, and I often wondered what the Station

Masters thought of such an arrangement. For wives especially, being married to both husband and job must have proved demanding. Not so Mrs Halstead; even on rest days she would warmly welcome any member of the staff, whatever the circumstances. Indeed, it was not uncommon for her to visit the booking office for a chat and a cup of tea. She took a great interest in the station and its staff, and we enjoyed her company.

Yet another visitor would be Mr Roe, Hough Green's Station Master. He would arrive each morning with takings from our smaller neighbour and accompany Mr Halstead to the bank. A pleasant and agile man, he always offered encouragement and enquired as to my welfare.

Thursdays were always eventful, as payday provided some hectic and emotional moments. To the porters, it was a day to cherish. The fact that they were paid weekly, as opposed to the clerks' fortnightly pay packet, meant that they could lend you a few pounds should the need arise. Not an unusual occurrence, as many clerks felt the pinch after the first week. It was also the day when retired railway employees visited the station to pay their rent or receive their pension.

Bill Kirk had many duties, including rents, paying bills and pensions. I soon became acquainted with many of the local characters. Their visits were often lengthy and they would talk about the old days and of characters dead or living. Photographs of their grandchildren would be produced and passed around. Listening to their amusing stories of yesteryear provided many funny moments. The elderly engine drivers especially would recall tales about driving in difficult conditions, having given a lifetime of service to the railway. These individuals were the 'old guard', having been masters of their trade, and it was sad that such skilled men would never again be required. The steam age was departing, and progress steamrolled onwards, destroying many traditions.

Naturally British Railways' rules and regulations were fair game for the audacious, who came in all shapes and sizes. The sight of a little old lady carrying a Yorkshire terrier in a shopping bag could be greeted with amusement. To suggest to such a person that a Zone Ticket (for the conveyance of bicycles and dogs by passenger train) was the order of the day could be interpreted as foolhardy. A wagging walk stick would be pointed at the brave soul, and the following tirade would ensue.

R.C.H. 60300

1st NOVEMBER, 1934.

(Reprint including Amendments authorised to operate not later than 31st December, 1947, and (see page 1) Notices of Increases of Charges).

_L M R_ RAILWAY.

BOOK OF RATES

APPLICABLE ONLY

TO

MERCHANDISE

BY

PASSENGER TRAIN OR OTHER SIMILAR SERVICE

FROM

_S P T H L_ STATION.

PART II.—SCALES AND CHARGES.

VOLUME 2

Printed by DEAN & CO. (Sept) Ltd., Stockport and London.

SCALES OF STANDARD CHARGES FOR MERCHANDISE BY PASSENGER TRAIN—*contd.*
GROUP S—Live Stock—*continued.*
SECTION (e) (G.5/(e))—*continued.*
Wild Animals in OWNER'S VANS, or on or in VEHICLES SPECIALLY PROVIDED—*continued.*

NOTE.—The Scale of Charges set out hereunder is compiled from the Standard Charges shown on preceding page and includes the 5 per cent. increase operative from 1st October, 1937.

Note.—*The following charges are subject to the addition of charges for Special Working in certain cases—See Book of Regulations—Reg. 46.*

Rate for conveyance, including station and service terminals at each end.

Miles.	Cubs of Wild Bears, Deer, Animals, Hyenas, Jackals, Lions, Monkeys, Sea-Lions, Pumas, Seals, Tigers, Tiger Cats. Wolves. In Owner's Vans, or in cages, crates, or boxes, on or in vehicles specially provided—per truck. (1)	Bears, Deer, Hyenas, Jackals, Lions, Sea-Lions, Seals, Tigers, Wolves. In Owner's Vans, or in cages or boxes, or on or in vehicles specially provided—per Animal. (2)	Camels, Elephants, Ostriches, Zebras. In horse boxes or vehicles other than specified in column 4—per Animal. (3)	Camels, Elephants, Ostriches, Zebras. In trucks specially strengthened, and in covered carriage trucks—per Animal. (4)	Miles.	Cubs of Wild Bears, Deer, Animals, Hyenas, Jackals, Lions, Monkeys, Sea-Lions, Pumas, Seals, Tigers, Tiger Cats. Wolves. In Owner's Vans, or in cages, crates, or boxes, on or in vehicles specially provided—per truck. (1)	Bears, Deer, Hyenas, Jackals, Lions, Sea-Lion, Seals, Tigers, Wolves. In Owner's Vans, or in cages or boxes, or on or in vehicles specially provided—per Animal. (2)	Camels, Elephants, Ostriches, Zebras. In horse boxes or vehicles other than specified in column 4—per Animal. (3)	Camels, Elephants, Ostriches, Zebras. In trucks specially strengthened, and in covered carriage trucks—per Animal. (4)

I have already touched briefly on my duties. Now I would like to go in to them in a little more detail. I think it is fair to say that the issuing of tickets and subsequent bookwork accounted for nearly 70 per cent of my time. This is only a generalisation, but I think that most clerks would agree with this figure. Many readers will have noted that every railway ticket carries a number. As well as being for audit purposes, this enabled the clerk to work out his ticket sales during his period of duty. He simply chalked up the first number of each specific series being sold, e.g. Liverpool Returns or Crewe Singles, and deducted the last number from the first. By this method he could work out how many tickets he had sold. Then, armed with a ready reckoner (no calculators in those days) and the Train Account Book, he would record all tickets sold to the various destinations at the end of his shift. The amount of cash taken should balance with the number

117 G.10

SCALES OF STANDARD CHARGES FOR MERCHANDISE BY PASSENGER TRAIN—*contd.*

GROUP 10. (G.10.)—

Corpses.

Ashes of Cremated Bodies, contained in a Coffin.

Note.—The Standard Charges set out hereunder are subject to an increase of 5 per cent. on and from 1st October, 1937.

Basis of Scale—for Scale, see below.

Description.	Rate for conveyance per mile. (Minimum charge as for 15 miles.)	Station Terminal at each end.	Service Terminals.	
			Loading.	Unloading.
	s. d.	s. d.	d.	d.
Without Hearse	1 6	Nil.	Nil.	Nil.
With Hearse (not Motor)	1 9	1 8	10	10
With Hearse (Motor)	1 9	1 8	10	10

Fractions of one penny in the total charge to be charged as one penny.

NOTE.—The Scale of charges set out hereunder is compiled from the Standard Charges shewn above and includes the 5 per cent. increase operative as from 1st October, 1937.

Note.—*The following charges are subject to the addition of charges for Special Working in certain cases—see Book of Regulations*—Reg. 46.

Rate for conveyance, including, where applicable, station and service terminals at each end.

Miles.	Without Hearse.	With Hearse (Motor and not Motor).	Miles.	Without Hearse.	With Hearse (Motor and not Motor).	Miles.	Without Hearse.	With Hearse (Motor and not Motor).	Miles.	Without Hearse.	With Hearse (Motor and not Motor).
	£ s. d.	£ s. d.		£ s. d.	£ s. d.		£ s. d.	£ s. d.		£ s. d.	£ s. d.
1 to 15	1 3 8	1 12 10	40	3 3 0	3 18 9	80	6 6 0	7 12 3	120	9 9 0	11 5 9
15¼	1 4 1	1 13 4	41	3 4 7	4 0 8	81	6 7 7	7 14 2	121	9 10 7	11 7 8
15½	1 4 5	1 13 9	42	3 6 2	4 2 6	82	6 9 2	7 16 0	122	9 12 2	11 9 6
15¾	1 4 10	1 14 3	43	3 7 9	4 4 4	83	6 10 9	7 17 10	123	9 13 9	11 11 4
			44	3 9 4	4 6 2	84	6 12 4	7 19 8	124	9 15 4	11 13 2
16	1 5 3	1 14 8	45	3 10 11	4 8 0	85	6 13 11	8 1 6	125	9 16 11	11 15 0
16¼	1 5 8	1 15 2	46	3 12 6	4 9 10	86	6 15 6	8 3 4	126	9 18 6	11 16 10
16½	1 6 0	1 15 7	47	3 14 1	4 11 8	87	6 17 1	8 5 2	127	10 0 1	11 18 8
16¾	1 6 5	1 16 1	48	3 15 8	4 13 6	88	6 18 8	8 7 0	128	10 1 8	12 0 6
			49	3 17 3	4 15 4	89	7 0 3	8 8 10	129	10 3 3	12 2 4
17	1 6 10	1 16 6									
17¼	1 7 3	1 17 0									
17½	1 7 7	1 17 5	50	3 18 9	4 17 2	90	7 1 9	8 10 8	130	10 4 9	12 4 2
17¾	1 8 0	1 17 11	51	4 0 4	4 19 0	91	7 3 4	8 12 6	131	10 6 4	12 6 0
			52	4 1 11	5 0 10	92	7 4 11	8 14 4	132	10 7 11	12 7 10
18	1 8 5	1 18 4	53	4 3 6	5 2 8	93	7 6 6	8 16 2	133	10 9 6	12 9 8
18¼	1 8 9	1 18 10	54	4 5 1	5 4 6	94	7 8 1	8 18 0	134	10 11 1	12 11 6
18½	1 9 2	1 19 3	55	4 6 8	5 6 4	95	7 9 8	8 19 10	135	10 12 8	12 13 4
18¾	1 9 7	1 19 9	56	4 8 3	5 8 2	96	7 11 3	9 1 8	136	10 14 3	12 15 2
			57	4 9 10	5 10 0	97	7 12 10	9 3 6	137	10 15 10	12 17 0
19	1 10 0	2 0 2	58	4 11 5	5 11 10	98	7 14 5	9 5 4	138	10 17 5	12 18 10
19¼	1 10 4	2 0 8	59	4 13 0	5 13 8	99	7 16 0	9 7 2	139	10 19 0	13 0 8
19½	1 10 9	2 1 1									
19¾	1 11 2	2 1 7									
			60	4 14 6	5 15 6	100	7 17 6	9 9 0	140	11 0 6	13 2 6
20	1 11 6	2 2 0	61	4 16 1	5 17 5	101	7 19 1	9 10 11	141	11 2 1	13 4 5
21	1 13 1	2 3 11	62	4 17 8	5 19 3	102	8 0 8	9 12 9	142	11 3 8	13 6 3
22	1 14 8	2 5 9	63	4 19 3	6 1 1	103	8 2 3	9 14 7	143	11 5 3	13 8 1
23	1 16 3	2 7 7	64	5 0 10	6 2 11	104	8 3 10	9 16 5	144	11 6 10	13 9 11
24	1 17 10	2 9 5	65	5 2 5	6 4 9	105	8 5 5	9 18 3	145	11 8 5	13 11 9
25	1 19 5	2 11 3	66	5 4 0	6 6 7	106	8 7 0	10 0 1	146	11 10 0	13 13 7
26	2 1 0	2 13 1	67	5 5 7	6 8 5	107	8 8 7	10 1 11	147	11 11 7	13 15 5
27	2 2 7	2 14 11	68	5 7 2	6 10 3	108	8 10 2	10 3 9	148	11 13 2	13 17 3
28	2 4 2	2 16 9	69	5 8 9	6 12 1	109	8 11 9	10 5 7	149	11 14 9	13 19 1
29	2 5 9	2 18 7									
30	2 7 3	3 0 5	70	5 10 3	6 13 11	110	8 13 3	10 7 5	150	11 16 3	14 0 11
31	2 8 10	3 2 3	71	5 11 10	6 15 9	111	8 14 10	10 9 3	151	11 17 10	14 2 9
32	2 10 5	3 4 1	72	5 13 5	6 17 7	112	8 16 5	10 11 1	152	11 19 5	14 4 7
33	2 12 0	3 5 11	73	5 15 0	6 19 5	113	8 18 0	10 12 11	153	12 1 0	14 6 5
34	2 13 7	3 7 9	74	5 16 7	7 1 3	114	8 19 7	10 14 9	154	12 2 7	14 8 3
35	2 15 2	3 9 7	75	5 18 2	7 3 1	115	9 1 2	10 16 7	155	12 4 2	14 10 1
36	2 16 9	3 11 5	76	5 19 9	7 4 11	116	9 2 9	10 18 5	156	12 5 9	14 11 11
37	2 18 4	3 13 3	77	6 1 4	7 6 9	117	9 4 4	11 0 3	157	12 7 4	14 13 9
38	2 19 11	3 15 1	78	6 2 11	7 8 7	118	9 5 11	11 2 1	158	12 8 11	14 15 7
39	3 1 6	3 16 11	79	6 4 6	7 10 5	119	9 7 6	11 3 11	159	12 10 6	14 17 5

[Continued.

An sample page from a Train Account Book from Mersey Road station, 1970. Ticket sales can be calculated from the 'commencing' and 'closing' numbers of the tickets issued on each day.

of tickets sold. If there was an error, the clerk had to begin the tedious job of checking all his ticket sales against the sum in the Train Account Book, as it may have been that he had forgotten to chalk up a particular sale. After carrying out all the stated procedures, and still failing to balance, he would enter the discrepancy under the surplus and loss in the Clerks' Settlement Book.

Once every two days the Traffic Book had to be balanced, in a similar process to the above, the clerk having to balance all ticket sales against the entries in the Train Account Book and the Settlement Book – a task not without its frustrations, as

RAILWAYS		CLERKS' SETTLEMENT BOOK						
DR.								
		SEASON TICKETS	EXCESS FARES	PARCELS & COLLECTED ROOMS		SUNDRIES		TOTAL
		£	£	£		Description	£	£

R Kelbrook	9 52	1 80						11.32
£ 11.32	9 52	1 80						11.32

R Kelbrook	11 12		0 03		11.15
£ 11.15	11 12		0 03		11.15
£ 22.47	20 64	1 80	0 03		
	1 83				

R Kelbrook	9 69		9.69
£ 9.69	9 69		9.69

R Kelbrook	9 16		9.16
£ 9.16	9 16		9.16
	1 6T		
£ 18.85	18 85		

R Kelbrook	11 42	0 06	11.48
	11 42	0 06	11.48

R Kelbrook	9 43		9.43
£ 9.43	9 43		9.43
	11 42		
£ 20.91	20 85	0 06	

A page from the Mersey Road station Clerks' Settlement Book,
May 1971.

any error brought about endless searching for his mistake, often with the help of a colleague. The Traffic Book had to balance, and often mistakes in the various procedures came to light.

The end of the month brought fresh endeavours, as the monthly receipts had to be compiled, again using the Traffic Book. This task could be as frustrating as the above, and you breathed a sigh of relief when the job had been completed.

I hope you have not found the above perplexing. I have described only the basics, and I can assure you that a booking clerk's job was an extremely complicated one, involving a great deal of bookwork and organisation.

One of the services that had ceased was that of forwarding luggage prior to travel, termed 'Passengers Luggage in Advance'. During the summer months people took advantage of this useful service, especially the elderly. Destinations on the South Coast, the Isle of Man and North Wales were popular, and Widnes, like most Lancashire towns, had its fair share of traffic. Most people consigned their luggage in the weeks prior to travel, and were grateful for the relief this service provided. Alas, it is no more, and modernisation has removed a feature of railway travel that was greatly appreciated.

Reserved sleeper or seat bookings were frequently handled by Miss Jo Donohue, part of the efficient reservation team. On receiving a request for reserved seats, we would immediately phone Lime Street and be given a seat number. Then we would simply transfer it onto a carbonised booking slip, the top copy going to the passenger and the carbon copy to Lime Street – a simple and effective system.

Dealing with timetable enquiries was reasonably straightforward, provided you could read timetables. Personally I always found the North Eastern Region difficult, but an aptitude in this field comes with experience and old hands could normally get you out of any tight spot.

Parcels traffic could provide a variety of headaches, especially when dealing with animals, as they often required special conditions and rates. Parcels were normally conveyed at 'owner's risk' or 'company risk', the latter costing more, as

British Railways bore the liability in the event of any damage or loss. The only parcels that were received at the station were those requiring collection, labelled 'TO BE CALLED FOR'. One of my duties was to phone the recipients of newly received parcels to inform them of their arrival. One particular pet shop in Widnes received mynah birds by this method, and I would immediately inform them on receipt, as the birds sometimes showed distress after spending long hours inside their small cardboard boxes. Sadly we occasionally received a dead one, while at other times the birds were just as lively, pecking away at the small air holes in their containers. Birds showing this sort of spirit where swiftly removed to the porters' room by Bart, who did his best to teach them a vocabulary of swear words.

These then were my basic duties, together with a few additional chores that I have failed to mention. Such was the variety of challenges. To use the classic phrase, I think 'never a dull moment' sums up the life of a busy booking clerk.

4
SOME LOCAL CHARACTERS

I would now like to digress from my story and introduce a couple of local characters, namely Eddie Meade and Brian Cassidy. The former was a driver at Widnes Motive Power Depot, coded 8D, and he related the following two stories.

An Edge Hill driver was working a Liverpool Lime Street to Bangor train during what was commonly known as the 'Big Freeze'. His fireman climbed on board with half a bottle of rum and immediately poured a liberal amount into their white enamel tea can, which at that time contained coffee. They were nicely warmed up when a station inspector unexpectedly climbed onto the footplate. Complaining that he was freezing, he requested a drink of tea. The driver replied that they had only got coffee, hoping no doubt that he would go away. To their complete surprise, he grabbed the can and helped himself.

'By God, that's good coffee – tastes of rum!' he exclaimed. 'Where did you get it?'

By this time his fireman was leaning out of the cab trying to control himself. The driver, thinking on his feet, replied that his wife had brought it from Kardoma and it was Jamaican. The inspector replied that he would get his wife to get some, before thanking him and departing. They had a good laugh and thought no more about it, but that was not the end of the story.

A fortnight later they were working the same train when the inspector spotted them, and climbed on board. Fortunately they only had tea brewing, as they had learned by their mistake.

'Where did you say you got that coffee from, driver?'

'The Kardoma,' he replied.

'Well, my wife went to get some and they didn't know what she was talking about.'

'Well I never,' muttered the driver. 'They must have made a mistake.'

The inspector departed and the footplate crew erupted in fits of laughter. The story would soon be the talk of Edge Hill shed, as everybody appreciated an amusing tale.

On another occasion a driver was working a train northwards from Crewe, the engine being an ex-works Class 5 with a speedometer. Now, speedometers were not that common, even on 'Black Fives', so the driver said to the fireman, 'Let's see how she goes,' and go they did! The engine steamed superbly and soon they were up to 80. Deciding to ease off, the driver tried to close the regulator, only to find it well and truly stuck. He and the fireman tried repeatedly to shut it, but to no avail. All the time their speed was increasing, and after a few minutes panic set in, and their efforts were more frantic than ever. They were doing well over 90mph when they finally closed the regulator, and immediately failed the engine at Warrington Bank Quay. Completely shaken, the crew found a convenient seat on the platform and sat down to unwind. Just at that moment the guard came up and raged at them for being madmen, as everything had come adrift in the brake. He flatly refused to go any further, asking to be relieved. While this commotion was going on, a passenger stepped forward and congratulated them on an exhilarating run. The guard nearly blew a fuse!

Brian Cassidy's railway career started as a trainspotter at Widnes South station. He soon started helping the porters to carry parcels, progressing to riding in the horse-drawn parcels van. When he was 15 Brian was offered a porter's job at Widnes South and found the work to his liking. On a Saturday night he often stayed with the signalman at Widnes No 7 box, to learn and observe. He recalled that the 11.05pm Liverpool Lime Street to Northampton mail train was so punctual that the locals use to set their clocks by it. Throughout the night the noise was constant, as the engines shunted in the various yards.

After working at Widnes South for a couple of years, he moved to Ditton Junction, again as a porter. His next move was to become a shunter, all traffic movements being carried out using oil lamps and a coupling stick, now a thing of the past. He

An unusual study by Brian Cassidy of a Class 8's coupling rods and valve gear at Deviation Sidings, Widnes, in 1966. *Brian Cassidy*

shunted every station in the Widnes area, and worked every yard. These were vast, and it is amazing to think that Widnes now only has one station and all the yards have gone. The freight line between Ditton and Warrington still clings to life but for how much longer? Many factories in the Widnes area employed their own shunting engines and their liveries brought a bit of colour to a mostly drab scene. Alas, they have all gone, which is a great pity.

Brian then moved to Garston (Speke) and Seaforth in the Liverpool area, enjoying his time at Speke 8C immensely. While he was working one of his passions was that of photographing steam locomotives, often with the aid of a box Brownie camera. After retirement he often turned up at the former LMS Club in Burnsall Street, Garston, to reminisce with other retired railwaymen. Sadly Brian has passed away, but he had a wonderful working knowledge of the various Widnes yards and stations. I

A Lourdes special crosses onto the slow line at Ditton Junction in 1960.
Brian Cassidy

miss his endless tales about his duties and experiences, some of which were funny in the extreme.

We had on the Cheshire Lines an antiquated internal telephone system, some of the phones resembling those seen in old Hollywood films. In some of the stations the operator would crank a small handle to bring it into use. Then, lifting the telephone, they would speak into the mouthpiece, simultaneously holding the earpiece.

I vividly remember being in the process of jotting down a message about lost property when I was interrupted by a rather impatient signalman – this was easily done, as anyone could interrupt or listen in, such was the system. He requested that I clear the telephone line as he had some urgent business with another box. I was reluctant to comply but, since the matter was urgent, I agreed. Being curious, I kept on the line while he made his call, whereupon he asked another signalman the result of the 3pm race at Haydock Park. Irritated, I told him what I thought of his urgent call, whereupon the signalman immediately replied that I was a nosey bastard, a remark repeated by the chorus of staff who were also listening in.

Listening in on this telephone circuit was commonly known as 'earwigging'. On nights it proved to be a great morale booster, as conversations could be held between various locations, and a new man could be nursed by his more experienced workmates. In truth, one never felt alone; however, it did hold certain disadvantages, as privacy was non-existent. We tended to hear about people's sex lives, and what they thought of their superiors. No doubt the bosses used the system to equal effect! 'Earwigging' could be an amusing and interesting pastime and is perhaps still used today by other nosey bastards who work on the railway.

On another occasion the phone rang, and was answered by Bart. A voice said that it was the Personnel Department, and asked, 'I am trying to trace a shag break. Do you have a shag break there?'

Bart was incredulous, before uttering the comment, 'Shag break? We don't even have a ruddy tea break!' and slammed the phone down.

As for the rest of us, we were too busy laughing. It was obviously a wind-up, perpetrated by a member of staff employed by British Railways comedy department.

At this point I would like to mention my Uncle Jim, who was a special class relief signalman on the Cheshire Lines. His career and background is perhaps typical of the now vanished breed of railwaymen, who gave years of loyal service to the various railway companies. Each man shared a special camaraderie with his workmates, and took a great pride in his job. Such a man was Jim's father, Daniel Downey, a Cheshire Lines engine driver based at Brunswick MPD. Like many railwaymen, he nursed his three sons towards a railway career, and could be reasonably satisfied when Jim and his brother Ron applied for railway service. It is worth mentioning that three of their cousins became drivers, thus keeping up the family tradition.

As a youngster Jim would dash down to Liverpool Central to meet his father, who often drove Sunday special excursions to such places as Cleethorpes or York. For these duties Dan was often supplied with a large locomotive and Jim would then ride back to the shed on the footplate of a 'B7' or 'K3'. Dan's regular engine, LNER 'D9' No 5104 *Queen Alexandra* had unwittingly become his mistress, and Jim's memory of his father's devotion to his engine remains paramount. Dan would visit the shed in his spare time, and help the fitters fix any offending component. Her cab pipework would be burnished often with Jim's assistance, and another young railwayman was being created. Having reached manhood, Jim tried unsuccessfully to obtain a position on the railway, but times were hard and vacancies rare. Eventually his father, after hearing a whisper of a forthcoming vacancy at Otterspool station, hastily informed his son, and Jim, spick and span, was waiting outside the Station Master's office the next morning The position was that of porter, and on seeing the Station Master Jim was offered the job for the princely sum of 38 shillings a week. I once asked him to describe his feelings on obtaining the position and he told me that no words could describe his elation. Thus Jim's career commenced at a small Cheshire Lines station in 1938.

His duties consisted of issuing and collecting tickets, polishing the brasswork and keeping the station in a state of cleanliness that would be unknown today. Other duties consisted of more operational tasks, the worst being that of priming the signal lamps on a bitterly cold day. This was not for the faint-hearted, as the ladders were often coated in ice. Jim had to be in full uniform, with polished buttons and shoes, and woe betide any man not up to scratch. Being ambitious he decided to become a signalman, and after training was rewarded with a signalman's position in Knotty Ash box on the former CLC in the autumn of 1939.

With the advent of the Second World War he found himself working the boxes at Knotty Ash and West Derby, and it was in the former that the following incident took place in 1941, a period often referred to as 'the May blitz'. In the middle of a raid Jim, on hearing a bomb whistling down towards the box, flung himself into his shelter, best described as an iron coffin. No sooner had he slammed the door when the bomb struck, blowing in all the windows and destroying a large part of the track. By good fortune, Knotty Ash box was built of stone, a rare occurrence on the cost-conscious CLC. Had it been wooden, it is doubtful whether Jim would have lived to tell his tale. On opening the door, Jim found it embedded with glass splinters and, although considerably shocked, he placed detonators on both running lines before walking to Knotty Ash station to raise the alarm. He arrived to find it deserted, so, finding a convenient table in the porters' room, he decided to rest.

The porter at Knotty Ash station that fateful night was Joe Foulkes, a man with whom I was to work in later years. On seeing an explosion in the box's general direction, Joe had feared the worst, and decided to investigate. His arrival at the box confirmed his worst fears, and a search for the missing signalman proved fruitless. With a heavy heart, he trudged wearily back to the station in the middle of the blackout to report the incident. By a twist of fate, the two men had passed one another in the blackout. On reaching the porters' room, he was greeted by the ghostly figure of Jim, rising up from the table, whereupon Joe fainted. Jim then had to move over, to make room for Joe, as it was debatable who had received the greatest shock that night.

In later years Jim served in several signal boxes, before being posted to Brunswick in 1948. This box had the distinction of being the first entrance/exit N.X. panel-operated box in Great Britain, the revolutionary system having been installed in February 1937. In 1955 he became a special class relief signalman, covering the Liverpool district of the old Cheshire Lines system until his transfer to former London & North Western territory in 1964, working Edge Hill power box and Liverpool Lime Street box before his retirement in 1975, after 37 years' service. I once asked him which was his most arduous duty, receiving the reply that Edge Hill's Exhibition Junction was one of the busiest.

Signalman Jim Downey works the UK's first 'NX' panel, installed in 1937, at Brunswick signal box in 1948. *Author's collection*

My signal box excursions greatly increased once I joined the railway. I had a lot to learn and the operating side was to me the most interesting and exhilarating, so I seldom missed an opportunity to spread my wings.

One night visit to see my uncle in Cressington box nearly ended in disaster. Fighting a stiff wind, I cycled in total darkness down the path running alongside the single track running from Cressington to Garston Church Road. A Stanier 8F was heaving and puffing towards me with a fitted freight, her lamps swaying as she rapidly closed. My dynamo barely functioned as I sought to gain speed and pass the approaching train. Suddenly I ran into an unseen signal cable, and landed with a thump right in the middle of the track, not more than 10 yards in front of the train. Painfully and with some haste, I picked myself up and limped with my cycle out of its path. Seconds later it wheezed by, the crew not even noticing me as I nursed my bruised legs. I had been lucky, and it was a rather ashen individual who arrived at the box, pushing a bicycle with a buckled front wheel. A mug of tea proved a godsend and I never made the same mistake again. Danger is ever present on any railway, and it is easy to come a cropper in seemingly normal circumstances.

Sadly most of my old haunts have vanished and the signal boxes are now just a fond memory. Even Liverpool Central has gone, and the high-level station is no more. One remembers the polished levers, brasswork and glowing coal fires. An atmosphere of warmth and welcome greeted you, and is little wonder that some signalmen treated their workplace as their second home. The boxes also contained numerous paperback books to keep the signalmen occupied during slack periods, as well as the mandatory stove and toilet. I must confess that I never saw a wireless set in any of the boxes I visited; as far as I am aware this was against regulations, as all distractions were strictly frowned upon.

Modern signalling has brought great changes to railway practice; a signalman can now control train movements within a 50-mile radius. However, I find this electronic wizardry dull and impersonal. Knobs have replaced levers and automatic signals control large stretches of track. The semaphore signal has virtually disappeared, replaced by the more efficient colour light signals. Perhaps the most incredible aspect of modern signal box construction is their apparent lack of windows. Today the signalman seldom sees the trains under his control, except as coloured lights on an illuminated panel.

Jim's brother Ron also became a signalman, and was for quite some years the regular bobby at Brunswick. One brother relieved the other, such was the family spirit on the old Cheshire Lines.

The old Widnes East signal box is seen on the day it closed in 1956.
Ron Downey

The accompanying photographs were taken by Ron on the closure of the old Widnes East box in 1956. On examination, one can see the stilts at the rear, supporting the box on the embankment. This method of construction was not uncommon on the CLC, but it did create problems. The box would sway as any train passed, and subsidence also led to difficulties. The old signal boxes at Halewood typified these problems: each leaned to a frightening degree and the movement created by passing trains had to be seen to be believed.

The second photograph (overleaf) shows the new box at Widnes East box, and its platelayers' hut. This hut was the scene of great mischief, as Ron soon learned the knack of leaping from the box window onto its flat roof, gaining access to the chimney. He would then smoke out the occupants, as he politely put it; however, he never said how the occupants retaliated. A good British Railways platelayer would never let such a prank go unpunished, as part of their training included antagonising signalmen and being missing when you wanted them.

The new box on its opening day in 1956 – note the platelayers' hut. Ron must have been quite athletic. *Ron Downey*

Sadly both brothers are deceased, and I have included a photograph of the pair taken inside Garston Church Road box shortly after Jim retired. A station once graced this location, but the tram and the car saw its demise. Sadly the box has also gone, and the traditional signal box has now been confined to history.

5

Brothers Jim and Ron Downey were photographed in Garston Church Road signal box in the early 1980s. *Author's collection*

The platelayer

The platelayer leads a lonely life,
Steel rails his companion, his child, his wife;
He walks close to nature which blossoms on banks,
Sees the wild flowers in gay coloured ranks,
Eyes ever searching the permanent way –
Such is his life, day after day.
Looking for faults, perhaps a cracked rail –
If undetected, a train could derail.
Checking the alignments, ballast and wear,
Eyeing the keys, checking each chair;
Perhaps a loose bolt, a fishplate or two,
Eyes always searching to protect me and you.
He walks beside ditches, rivers and streams,
Ever attentive, seldom to dream;
Summer and winter, ah, the hardest of all:
The weather gets colder as leaves start to fall.
Frost, snow and fog, all part of the job,
He'll still walk his section, onward he'll plod
To shiver and cough and dream of his fire,
The warmth of his cabin by the old rambling briar.
Stopping a while he'll watch the proud hawk
Silently circling, its prey it does stalk.
He admires this hunter with accurate eye –
Down drops the hawk and something will die!
Perhaps they're both hunters, two of a kind,
Keen eyes ever searching this section of line,
But one to save life, the other brings death,
A strange combination, he thinks, whilst at rest.
Eyes like a hawk, he'll always need those,
For a railwayman essential, as the platelayer knows.

Barry Allen

The old signalman's reunion

He never noticed the wind on his face,
Nor the rain as it fell as if with God's grace;
He just stared at the spot where his signal box stood
And his mind went back to that metal and wood.
No trace of it now, just a bare patch of ground,
Nor the clatter of levers – how he longed for that sound.
For twenty-five years he'd worked at that spot,
Content with his living, content with his lot.
Now in retirement he turns to thoughts of his past –
Two lines are missing, the down and up fast.
The wind gently moans as if in despair;
He looks to the heavens – it doesn't seem fair.
He remembers the joy of this spot as a lad
As he walks through ruins so silent and sad.
Once there was pride on this lonely old line
That nature's reclaiming, perhaps for all time.
He turns up his collar, returns to the road,
Looking his years, feeling so old.
He won't come again, he'll live on his dreams;
Nothing, it appears, stays at it seems.
Time waits for no man, he always said that.
He'll return to the loneliness of his pensioner's flat.
He turns again, one final farewell,
Imagines the tinkle of the old box's bell.
He never noticed the wind on his face,
Nor the rain as it fell as if with God's grace.
He just stared at the spot where his signal box stood
And his mind went back to that metal and wood.

Barry Allen

JOE AND BART GET RATTY

After two months' training Mr Halstead suggested that I take a turn on the late shift, as the experience would do me good. The evening shift offered a nice change from the daily bustle, and was lot quieter. I would be working with Bart and Joe, so I was guaranteed a few laughs. I wondered what their reaction would be when they discovered that I was working lates, and I did not have to wait long before I found out.

On my first night Joe requested that I fetch coal for the booking office fire, so, being obliging, off I went clutching the coal bucket. It was nearly pitch black when I reached the coalhole, the station gas lamps only emitting a dull flickering glow. Widnes North had changed little since the Victorian era, its modernisation plans lost in the annals of time. It was very atmospheric, and I opened the coalhole door cautiously, half expecting Bart to come leaping out. After determining no one was inside, I relaxed and, bending down, proceeded to shovel coal into the bucket. Suddenly a dark form jumped over my shoulder, giving me one hell of a fright. For a second I thought my imagination had run riot, such was the speed of the object. Still, I was very uneasy and decided to return to the booking office for a lamp before proceeding further.

Walking back, I spotted Joe and Bart in a huddle, so knew that my experience had been real and somehow they were responsible. It came to me in a flash – one of them must have put a cat in the coal place shortly before my arrival. On reaching the grinning pair, I enquired as to the identity of the comedian, stating that I did not think putting a cat in the coal place at 9.30 at night a particularly funny event. Bart's expression changed to one of sheer surprise and he pointed up the platform. I was just in time to see a large rat amble through a gap in the fence. Completely shocked, I angrily stated that the joke was in poor taste, and pointed out that I could have been bitten, whereupon the pair sheepishly apologised. Bart was still puzzled as to why I had thought it a cat. In truth, I never dreamed that they would get up to such a trick. Joe later explained that Bart had chased the creature around the platform before trapping it in the coalhole. Only later had they thought up the plot, and never considered the implications. To them, it was just another prank.

Now, I have already mentioned that a certain clerk was not fond of mice. Well, I was working with him on the late shift when Bart breezed into the booking office whispering that he had just placed a dead mouse in his lunch box. I felt tense, and was dying to laugh, even though it was a wicked joke. As it was nearly time for our break, the clerk unwrapped his sandwiches, watching us closely. He suspected that something was going on, after seeing Bart whisper in my ear and my subsequent expression. Still, it would not put him off eating his food, as he had visions of pumping me for information after our break. How I kept a straight face I'll never know – I was so tense that I wanted to pass water. I held on as Bart and the clerk chatted about horses, while every now and again the latter would shoot an enquiring glance in my direction. Bart was outwardly quite normal, his face portraying no sign of emotion.

When the clerk had finished his sandwiches, he started rummaging in his bag for his desert, an act that made me turn my back, as by now I had developed a broad grin. After composing myself, I turned to find him feeling a paper package in his lunch box. Unrolling it, he stated that his wife must have put in a extra treat for him. This was too much for me, and I exploded into laughter just as the dead mouse emerged. He was completely transfixed at the sight of the dead creature. Bart and I were in convulsions, tears streaming down our faces as he let loose a torrent of abuse. Throwing us out of the booking office, it took quite a while for him to forgive us, and who could blame him? Still, he laughed about the incident some weeks later, accepting it as a wicked joke; however, we noticed that he was always cautious on future occasions when opening his lunch box.

Passenger censuses were not exactly rare, and like all good

trunk routes the CLC was selected for such treatment during the month of August. This resulted in a grade three clerk being sent with management blessing to probe our receipts. This young man spent hours peering into books while continually clicking his ballpoint pen out of sheer boredom. He would jump at the chance to sell a ticket, and such a mundane task brought him great joy. Thank goodness I did not have to work in the Passenger Manager's office, whatever the grading. For our part, we had to count the number of people leaving and departing. The task was at times chaotic, especially at peak periods. Tommy would only count the passengers and never the railway workers with free passes. As we had a fair number of the latter, the whole exercise was rather pointless. Things really got out of hand when Bart counted a pregnant lady as two passengers, and the mind boggles as to the eventual figures. Quite honestly the whole thing was poorly conducted from the start, as to carry out a survey when many passengers were absent during the holiday period was a trifle suspicious. Railwaymen are not stupid, and the expression 'it takes one to know one' would not be amiss.

Widnes North had originally been called Farnworth, but due to the constant confusion with the other Farnworth near Bolton, it was renamed Widnes North. Billy Marriott, a former Brunswick fireman, told me that after the war Farnworth's booking clerk, Jimmy McCloud, regularly asked permission to fire their 'D9' or 'D10' into Liverpool Central or vice versa. Apparently he was an excellent fireman and Bill was quite happy to let this young man perform the task. This was unusual, and the clerk perhaps had footplate aspirations, but unfortunately I cannot tell you if he succeeded.

Years earlier Farnworth had been the scene of a tragic accident. The station's geographical location alongside a road bridge had prompted the planners to dismiss the idea of spanning the platforms with a footbridge as an unnecessary expense. For many passengers this meant an anxious dash across the road bridge if they had chosen the wrong platform. For the elderly and disabled it was especially difficult and indeed time-consuming. I heard the story from my Uncle Jim, as his father was a key witness at the inquiry.

To the best of my knowledge the victims were a woman and child. Their unexpected arrival on the Liverpool platform to catch a Manchester train caused some concern, as a Liverpool-bound train was at the platform ready to depart. Its driver, Dan Downey, was waiting for the tip from the guard and watched the events unfold. The woman asked if it was the Manchester train, only to be told that the Manchester train was imminent, but on the other platform. Suddenly she started to panic. Pushing a pram, she began to run to the back of the train just as the Manchester was approaching on the adjacent line. Dan desperately tried to warn her of the danger, as he could see what was about to happen. Sadly the woman either never heard his cries or chose to ignore them. Frantically she pushed her pram across the sleeper crossing, straight in front of the arriving train. She and her child were both killed instantly, and Dan had to attend the subsequent inquest. The accident had a great effect on him, and his sons said that he was never quite the same man again. Ironically, Widnes North, or just Widnes as it is known today, now has a footbridge, although not as a the result of the accident; it materialised once they closed the eastbound booking office. The dash over the road bridge is now a thing of the past, and at last we have a little progress.

Although my worship of the iron horse remained paramount, an encounter with the four-legged variety proved an unexpected surprise, especially at 6.30 in the morning. My daily ritual was to rise at 6.00am, have a quick wash and shave, then creep down the stairs so as to not wake my parents. On reaching the kitchen, the dog, ever alert, would look up, grunt, sigh, roll on his back and stick his legs in the air. Humans should let sleeping dogs lie. After a quick cup of tea, it was off to the bus for Garston. Imagine my surprise when, on opening the front door, I found a beady eyed horse standing in the path. I recall rubbing my eyes, thinking I was dreaming. A bridle dangled enticingly, so I reached for it in an effort to capture the runaway. The horse would have none of it, and backed down towards the open drive gates. I gave chase, only to meet a policeman pedalling furiously up the hill.

The horse had escaped from a convent and he was in hot pursuit. The fugitive had other ideas, and watched the constable with a knowing eye. As soon as he got near, it galloped off, leaving behind a swearing cyclist, wondering why he had joined the police force. Unfortunately I did not have time to watch the pantomime, but what a tale to tell on reaching work. Quite naturally most of the station staff disbelieved my story except for Tommy. He said I was probably telling the truth, as he had once encountered an elephant sitting on his front step. Thank goodness someone believed me. As for my parents, the hoof prints told all, and it was a great pity that the others had not witnessed such an amusing interlude.

My probationary period was drawing rapidly to a close and my final late shift once again proved eventful.

Widnes was the base for a minor invasion of Indian salesmen, who arrived each morning from Manchester and returned later in the day. By a strange twist I found myself working with relief porter Joe Foulkes, who had survived his ghostly encounter with my uncle during the Second World War. He had just been paid, and we found ourselves standing on the platform near a group of salesmen who were waiting to return home. Joe was staring at his unopened pay packet when he was spotted by one of the salesmen. He immediately joined us, opened his case, and pulled out a shirt. Waving it in front of Joe's face, he exclaimed that it could be his for just 30 shillings – good value, as it was British, none of your foreign rubbish. Joe was wary, and reluctant to part with his money. Seeing his uncertainty, the salesman rapidly reduced the price to £1, which resulted in Joe ripping open his pay packet and handing over the money. The salesman then commented that Joe was a very crafty man and would not regret his purchase.

Having dealt with Joe, he now turned his attention to me, holding up ties of various colours and stating that they were a real bargain at 6 shillings. I told him that I had only 3s 6d in my pocket, plus my bus fare home. Since I had no desire to walk, I declined his offer. This brought about a renewed effort, but once again I repeated my financial status. However, one of the ties had taken my fancy and it must have shown. It was magically produced once again with an asking price of 5 shillings. Again I offered 3s 6d, just as the salesman's train appeared. Suddenly he thrust the tie at me and demanded my three and six, stating that I was a cheeky boy, a sentiment no doubt endorsed by my mother. On boarding he was still muttering about me to his colleagues, much to my amusement.

The following Saturday I found myself standing in front of Derek Halstead who stood pensively holding a piece of paper. The summons had been sudden, and I was ushered into the booking office. It all seemed very official, and I felt increasingly anxious. However, a beaming Mr Halstead shook my hand, informing me that as from the following Monday I was to be transferred to West Allerton station on the former LMS system. I had passed my probationary period and was now an official grade four booking clerk. Needless to say the news came as real shock. Naturally I had expected a transfer, but the suddenness of it took me by surprise. There would not be time to say goodbye to all my colleagues, and I left with mixed feelings, as in many ways I was sorry to go. Tommy Connor quipped that the LMS was not much of railway, even after electrification. Old rivalries still prevailed, and a Cheshire Lines man was proud of his heritage. The former LNER route encompassing the old CLC lines provided a crisp and punctual service. I would find a big difference, he bleated, adding to my apprehension. I waved goodbye and boarded the diesel railcar for Garston and home. This would be my final journey and my mind was already focused on my new posting. I wondered if my new position would be as entertaining as my last; Bart and Joe in particular, had provided some memorable moments and had been a pleasure to work with. A fresh opportunity beckoned as slowly Widnes North disappeared from view and I said goodbye to the CLC.

6
WEST ALLERTON

Naturally excited, I blurted out the news to my parents, who were pleased that I had passed my training period and made the grade. Equally my new posting was just under a mile from my home, so there was no need to rise at such an ungodly hour, or so I thought.

On my first morning I anxiously jumped on my bike and pedalled furiously to West Allerton station. Entering the booking office after a cautious knock, I encountered Philip Murphy, the young booking clerk. He received my news with growing dismay, becoming utterly dejected. Apparently he had been informed of his pending transfer, but now that the moment had arrived he did not want to leave. I felt sorry for him, as this clearly was a nice posting, and modernisation did have its benefits.

A mess room adjoined the booking office, and was aptly named, being strewn with chairs, magazines and paperback books. It did, however, provide a wonderful surprise, as a large picture window overlooked all the running lines. To an ex-trainspotter, this was indeed a bonus. I quickly noticed a Belling stove and electric kettle, a far cry from my previous posting with its gas cooker and lighting. This would be like home from home and just a whisker away.

West Allerton station had been built in 1939, so was fairly new, even predating modernisation, and was constructed to cater for the new housing estates that were rapidly encroaching into the area. The LMS had been keen to grow commuter traffic and saw it as a good business opportunity. Unfortunately the Second World War put a damper on things and the station never quite achieved its potential. Its main claim to fame were its three long platforms, built to deal with excursion traffic that never materialised. The three platforms served four running lines, up and down fast and up and down slow, each platform having a waiting room and flower beds. One downside was that the waiting rooms had no fires, due to their timber and hardboard construction. This resulted in passengers milling around in the booking office corridor until their train was sighted. This could be an annoying practice, as in the winter the corridor would become congested, with any delays leading to increasing demands as to the whereabouts of the train. This was an accepted part of the job, but things sometimes got out of hand, with passengers continually requesting fresh information every few minutes, even after an update. Another problem arose once their train had been sighted, with the passengers strolling to join it, frequently causing delays, much to the annoyance of the guards.

The main building was situated on the railway bridge in Booker Avenue. Wymans had newspaper shop as part of the station complex and sold *Playboy* magazine; this provided the porters with an excuse to polish the counter in exchange for a loan. The bookstall had the cleanest counter for miles, and we

Platforms 2 and 3 at West Allerton in 1963. An electric multiple unit is about to depart for Liverpool Lime Street. *Author's collection*

were the happiest porters. The station building also offered a panoramic view of the crossroads and avenue. We could even observe the rival bus route.

An unusual feature appeared on the bank above Platform 1, namely a tribute to Merseyside's former titled expresses, the 'Merseyside Express', 'Shamrock', 'Red Rose' and 'Manxman'. Built by former porter Lenny Lees, this concrete structure was a fitting reminder of those prestige workings. Only a few photographs remain of this prominent structure, as it has now completely disappeared. Another of his creations is seen in the accompanying photograph, showing his amazing ability. He was

In the late 1950s porter Leonard Lees proudly displays one of his artistic creations at West Allerton station, Liverpool. He was a popular member of staff and highly talented, as the photo clearly demonstrates. West Allerton station contained another of his creations, located on the bank alongside Platform 1; titled 'Four star turns', it was a fitting tribute to the prestigious titled expresses that served the city, and was familiar to the local railway fraternity. *Liverpool Daily Post*

clearly a most talented individual and was acknowledged in the BR fraternity for his creativity.

My hours were 7.30am till 2.45pm five days a week, and on Saturdays I finished earlier. With the arrival of electrification in the early 1960s many stations were rebuilt or modernised; West Allerton endured the latter in a bid to attract the public to the benefits of electrification. Our local diesel and electric train services were quite numerous, with trains to Lime Street, Crewe, Runcorn and Chester, together with various steam workings. The highlight was the 8.05am to Bangor, often hauled by a 'Britannia' 'Pacific'. Peak hours provided plenty of activity, especially between 8.00 to 8.30am, our mad half-hour, with steam, diesel and electric trains arriving and departing to various destinations. Goods traffic was in the main steam-hauled, and I enjoyed the sight of 'Crabs', 'Black Fives', Stanier 8Fs, 'WDs' and Standard 9Fs bustling along with various loads. Perhaps steam would go on forever!

Once peak hour was over, things slowed down and I would polish the brass and booking office counter, although my first job was to make sure that the dating press was correct. One of the things that I instigated was the procurement of an additional ticket rack; electrification had brought improvements and our passenger figures had greatly increased.

The station staff consisted of yours truly, two porters, Johnny Wakeham and another individual whose name escapes me. This latter gentleman was only in the job for a couple of weeks before he was transferred, as he had trouble getting out of bed. His replacement, Martin Parker, hailed from Kilkenny, one of many Irishmen making a living working for British Railways in the Liverpool area.

On my first morning the Station Master wanted to see what sort of clerk had been sent by the Passenger Manager's office. Neville Squires was one of the youngest Station Masters on British Railways, and was quick-witted and likeable. Fortunately we were very compatible, and became good friends. I was particularly sorry when he was promoted some months later. All the station staff were comparatively young, but we

In 1964 the author sports a new haircut at West Allerton.
Author's collection

The author fools about with Martin Parker at West Allerton in 1963.
Author's collection

Johnny Wakeham and the
author at West Allerton
in 1963. *Author's collection*

quickly blended to become a team. Luckily I had landed on my
feet, and it turned out to be a most interesting position.

After a couple of days I had familiarised myself with my new
surroundings and things became more routine. Much to the
porter's dismay, I introduced an improved version of the train
book and on recept of the additional rack, altered the ticket
layout to allow more space for special cheap day returns. These
tickets represented good value, being cheaper than ordinary
singles, hence an increase in sales. We always mentioned that
they were the cheaper option, and this advice was naturally
gratefully received. When I arrived we had no printed Liverpool
special cheap day returns, having sold out some weeks
previously. It was quite a task to write scores of blank card
tickets for Liverpool for an impatient queue of punters. Quickly
I remedied the situation, and we never again ran out of tickets.

A frequent visitor was Constable Alan Wood, who would arrive on his scooter early in the morning for his tea and toast. In his early 20s and full of wit, he often related stories about his escapes on and off the beat. His main complaint regarded the 'lollypop' pedestrian crossing personnel, who, being elderly, succumbed to any ailment, particularly in bad weather. By going off sick they created a job that he clearly did not appreciate. We were always glad to see Alan, as his stories and curses made our day. Sometimes he would arrive blowing his top due to some frustrating incident, proving that policemen are human after all.

One of our passengers was none other than Mr Smith, Liverpool's Chief Constable. This popular gentleman would enter the booking office to chat about various topics, including the timekeeping of his train. It was this habit that led to a rather amusing incident with PC Wood. One morning Alan arrived earlier than usual, with his tongue hanging out! He entered the mess room with Martin, and was just about to close the door when he cried, 'God, it's Smithy!' whereupon he promptly slammed it. Unfortunately Alan had left his police helmet on the booking office table, so I desperately tried to remove it just as Mr Smith entered the booking office. Sadly I was unsuccessful, so I tried to hide it by sitting on the table.

Mr Smith was now in the booking office and immediately asked me what size I took in police crash helmets. Seeing my embarrassment, he smiled and suggested that if I opened the mess room door we could see if his train was approaching. Alan was clearly shaking by now, but Mr Smith was having fun, and had not finished with his subordinate. Unexpectedly he strolled past me and turned the knob a couple of times before releasing it. Then he tapped on the door, and said, 'Look, I know you are in there. I was young myself once. However, the public do not take kindly to my men hanging around stations drinking tea when they are on duty. If by any chance you should ever return, don't advertise the fact by leaving your police helmet and scooter lying around for all the world to see.'

Fully satisfied, he turned and winked at me before leaving

LNER Class 'K3' passing Mersey Road with an Up Liverpool to Hull service in 1938. Driver Harry Grieve claims these locos helped win the war! *James Stone* (See Chapter 11 for more of James Stone's pictures)

the office. Martin claimed that when Mr Smith turned the knob Alan went pale, looking quite ill. To his credit, he never returned at that time again, but still managed to put in the odd appearance, as nothing could put Alan off his tea and toast. Nevertheless, that day I witnessed a lesson in diplomacy, and one that Alan would never forget. Mr Smith was quite a character and was always welcome.

Mr Manton, another regular commuter, was, so we were informed, Edge Hill's Yard Master, and was the only person using the station with a 1st Class railway pass. Tall, friendly and polite, he always wore traditional railway manager's railway apparel, namely a long black mackintosh and bowler hat. Even at the birth of the 1960s Edge Hill still had vast goods yards, not to mention its famous 'grid iron' marshalling yard, which was world famous, hence the importance of his position.

Mossley Hill, the next station north towards Liverpool, suddenly acquired a British Railways bicycle to allow the Station

Whoops! This amusing photo shows a 1980s mishap at Edge Hill with a Class 47 loco – which was recovered and found to be undamaged. *Author's collection*

Master to journey to and from his home. This cycle was greatly welcomed by the staff as they could reach the pub in record time. However, this displeased the boss, so the cycle was locked up, only to reappear outside the pub, especially when he wasn't around. Now and again the Station Master would cycle to West Allerton station. The bike would suddenly appear round the corner with Neville peddling like mad, with his pipe blazing. This was a comical sight, as the cycle was rather small, and Neville rather tall, and when in full flight it reminded us of the 'Royal Scot' attacking Beattock Bank. I cannot recall what happened to the cycle, but it is rumoured that it was donated to the Science Museum at Kensington.

In conjunction with the St John Ambulance Association, British Railways ran first aid courses for its employees, mainly in the evening. This resulted in the combined staff from Mossley Hill and West Allerton attending a course at Runcorn Goods Depot under the wing of Morris Williams, all of us having volunteered at the Station Master's request. Morris was real character, employed as Runcorn's yard master, and not far off retirement age. Completely experienced, he had performed most railway tasks, including that of Station Master; however, his great interest in life was teaching first aid.

Our initial trip consisted of Mr Squires, Martin Parker, yours truly and Taffy Williams, one of the porters from Mossley Hill. Having duly assembled, the Station Master told us that our railway passes had not yet arrived, a factor of little importance as he would explain the circumstances to the staff at Runcorn. Unknown to us, Scotsman Jimmy Fulton, one of Mossley Hill's booking clerks, had other ideas, and soon the telephone was buzzing between the two stations.

On alighting at Runcorn station, we allowed all the passengers to leave before approaching the barrier, only to be confronted by a burley railway policeman. Neville requested that we leave all the talking to him, which led to a brief and confident explanation – and our arrest. In a serious manner we were informed that we were to be charged with fare evasion and impersonating railway employees, leaving us speechless. Our Station Master's pipe was smoking heavily by this time as we pleaded our innocence; however, the policeman said that he had received a tip-off, and we immediately guessed its source. This was too much for us, so once again we pleaded our case. Suddenly the policeman burst out laughing, clearly enjoying the wind-up. We did likewise and it is a wonder that Jimmy's ears weren't burning as we called him a few choice names.

We quickly found out that the first part of the course consisted of a series of lectures on the human anatomy, often accompanied by charts containing all the necessary illustrations. This was not for the squeamish, and I continually fidgeted in my seat. The Station Master got the hiccups and another of our party broke wind. All distractions were completed ignored by the Scottish doctor, who droned on, clearly wanting the lessons to finish on time. Later we came to the practical side, consisting of bandage applications. This led to a funny episode, the Station Master suffering at the hands of his subordinates.

It was our habit to proceed to the nearest public house

The St. John
Ambulance Association

BRITISH RAILWAYS
AMBULANCE CENTRE
LONDON MIDLAND REGION

This is to Certify that

Barry Allen

has successfully passed an

EXAMINATION IN FIRST AID

In the month of March, 1963
at

Runcorn

J. E. L. Quaite   *Philip Sattwed.*

Secretary OF THE MOST VENERABLE   *Director General*

Valid for 3 years from the date shewn hereon

My BR First Aid Certificate, 1963.

once the session was over, before catching a train home. Morris Williams asked for a volunteer for bandaging practice and our Station Master promptly obliged. Inviting Neville to sit in a chair, Morris demonstrated a bandaging application and invited us to follow suit, while he popped out for a few minutes. The Station Master sat patiently while we applied bandages, until he was securely tied to the chair. A cry of alarm went out, but it was too late. He was now well and truly trussed up. Leaving him thus, we departed to the pub, amid threats of suspensions and sackings. As the knots had not been unduly tightened, we expected him to break free within minutes and follow us to the pub.

Eagerly we awaited his arrival with glee but, as the minutes passed and he failed to show, a more sombre mood prevailed. Deciding to return, we were confronted by Morris, who swiftly reprimanded us for our actions. Morris had freed Neville on his return, the Station Master's struggling having only tightening the knots. What made things worse was his desire to pass water, so it had been a painful experience. He took the joke in tremendous spirit and immediately sacked the lot of us. He never volunteered again, not even for the mouth-to-mouth resuscitation, featuring a distinctly female-looking dummy. Needless to say, we all had a go at that. We enjoyed many laughs on the course and it was to Morris's credit that we all passed with a high degree of proficiency. Even today I still have my certificate and retain the original first aid manual for sentimental reasons.

7
THE 'BIG FREEZE', 1962-63

Many readers will remember the bad winter of 1962/63, one
that earned a place in history books, being popularly termed
the 'Big Freeze'. During this period the train services were a
trifle chaotic; in fact, many trains never ran at all. Looking out
of the mess room window, it was not unusual to see a London
express headed by a Type 4 diesel with a steam engine in tow,
the latter supplying steam for the carriage heating or rending
additional assistance.

Our services suffered accordingly as the relentless cold
took a hold. The new electric multiple units were not without
teething problems and one could well imagine their demise
at the advent of the cold spell. Everything froze, points, stock,
locomotives and the passengers, who would stamp their feet,
muttering curses when their train failed to appear on time. One
particular morning proved unforgettable, as all hell broke loose
due to a series of disasters.

At about 7.30am a late-running electric multiple unit
arrived at Platform 4 for Liverpool Lime Street. Immediately
there was a loud bang, followed by the dying whine of motors.
Looking through the window I saw the driver leave his cab
and, joined by the guard, ask everybody to leave the failed
train. Grudgingly the passengers made their way up the steps
towards the booking hall. Fortunately there were not too
many disgruntled faces and I saw John Wakeham informing
them of the time of the next train to Liverpool. As they had
more than half an hour to wait, most decided to mill around
in the booking hall, just to keep warm. I was in the process
of telephoning Traffic Control when the driver entered and
informed them of our problem. He then asked permission to
cook his breakfast on our electric stove, after being informed
that a steam engine would be dispatched to tow away the

offending train, but it was not expected for at least half an hour. Thankfully we still had the down fast opened to Liverpool. So far, so good!

Soon the driver had the frying pan sizzling and the smell of bacon filled the booking office and hall. After enquiring as to his favourite steam loco, I was handed a bacon sandwich, probably to shut me up, the conversation having swung to his home town of Crewe. By now new passengers were arriving for the next train, and it was soon sighted, much to my relief. A mass of passengers descended the steps leading to Platform 2 and boarded the electric unit. No sooner had the guard received the tip than the motors expired, and the grim-faced driver made his way up the steps watched by several angry passengers. I could not believe my eyes – it was a chance in a thousand that two electric trains would fail simultaneously blocking both lines into Liverpool. Our bacon munching driver was equally astonished, and went to assist his colleague. In the meantime, I was to again telephone Traffic Control and tell them of our latest calamity.

Some passengers had left the train and were hammering on the window asking for their money back. John, on the receiving end of much verbal abuse, retired to the mess room, leaving me to face the music. It was a torrid period when suddenly a miracle materialised as the unit's motors burst into life. The two drivers had cured the fault, and the train was ready to go. We all breathed a sigh of relief when it departed, 10 minutes late, jam-packed and steaming. Beaming, the first driver returned and settled down to finish his well-earned, if belated, breakfast. Soon a 'WD' steam locomotive was sighted, approaching the stranded train, whereupon our driver said goodbye and left, clutching a round of toast for the guard. We never saw him again, but he had truly saved our bacon, while I had eaten his!

I have many memories of that winter, but the above remains paramount. I do not think the toilets worked for several weeks and we were forced to use the public house down the road, much to the porters' delight. Even in one of the severest winters on record we coped. Somehow the trains got through and the benefits of steam triumphed over diesel. As for the travelling public, they generally took it in their stride, suffering like the rest of us as the Siberian conditions continued. What would happen today if we experienced similar conditions? Enough said – I leave you with your thoughts!

One morning I arrived to find two policemen waiting for me, and I immediately saw that we had experienced a break-in. The booking office window had been smashed and Martin was busy trying to clear up the mess. Unfortunately the two constables reiterated that nothing should be disturbed until the CID arrived, which as you can guess presented problems. They first asked if anything was missing and, on checking, everything appeared to be in order.

Later the CID were busy inspecting pieces of broken glass for prints, with little success. Passengers were arriving continually, leading to brief explanations and an increasing queue. I was glad when the peak hour was over. However, glass had managed to find its way into every available corner. For elimination purposes Martin and I had our fingerprints taken, with a singular lack of enthusiasm. The police's theory was that the criminals were trying to gain access to Wymans, but that was open to debate. After going through all their various procedures, they departed leaving us to clear up the mess. A carpenter arrived from Edge Hill to board up the window, and this was no sooner said than done. Sadly I have forgotten his name; however, he later made quite an impression on me. Having boarded up the window, he decided to have his dinner, and as we talked the subject of rats arose, and he related the following story.

During the war he had been a military policeman, and was dispatched to Liverpool Central in the early hours to meet a horsebox special. The train was late, so he decided to kill time by strolling around the city centre. Having reached Lord Street, he encountered an elderly policeman who cycled towards him shouting, 'Rats, rats! Quick lad – let's get up the nearest lamp post!'

Using the bicycle for support, they scrambled up a

convenient lamp and, on kicking the bike away, sat there in frozen silence. Suddenly an enormous army of rats poured down the street, led by the biggest rat he had ever seen. There were literally thousands, and once they had passed the shaken pair climbed down. The old bobby said that the docks had just been bombed, and the rats were looking for a safer haven. Now I have heard stories from old dockers who claimed that rats frequently left the docks before an air raid. One can only speculate as to the truth of these stories; however, one thing is certain. As he related his story the horror of that night was etched on his face, and it had clearly been a most frightening experience.

I wonder what the carpenter would have said if I had told him that West Allerton had rats. We often heard them scampering about in the cellar, and we would stamp on the floor in a bid to scare them off. When they persisted, we would grab a shovel and race to the cellar only to find that they had vanished. After a while their constant pattering got to us, so we called in the railway rodent operative, who arrived with some rat poison and did the necessary. Still the bait seemed to have no effect, and on late turn this was particularly disturbing; as Martin used to complain, they were keeping him awake! The cellar was also full of old posters, advertising excursions to famous holiday locations or depicting scenes of popular seaside resorts. Some had been issued by the LMS and to Martin's eyes completely worthless. Being a good porter he burned them, thus creating more space. Today those posters would be worth a fortune, but back in the 1960s they were ten a penny, and the magic words 'if only' spring to mind.

The carpenter was to return, as we were minus one paying-in window, and the plywood substitute proved troublesome. In the meantime a ticket audit was necessary, to ensure that none had been stolen. As we literally stocked hundreds, a clerk was dispatched post-haste to carry out this tedious chore. Enter George Hignett, the most unforgettable character I ever met.

George appeared to be in his 50s and, if memory serves me correctly, was a native of St Helens, possessing a strong accent and a humorous disposition. It did not take him long to make an impression, as he knew all the characters working on the railway. Being on relief enabled him to travel around, so he was a mine of information concerning the staff at most locations. George would relate humorous tales endlessly, and would soon have you in hysterics, making it extremely difficult to concentrate on the task in hand.

One of his stories concerned the war, when he was a naval gunner. According to George, he was taking a shower when a U-boat surfaced quite close to his ship. Completely naked, he ran to his gun only to find that the U-boat had dived. As the temperature was well below zero, his backside quickly became frozen to the deck. Now I was getting a bit dubious by this time, especially when he mentioned dodging icebergs in the Irish Sea. George then went on to explain that old seamen knew when a ship was doomed, once they saw rats performing lifeboat drill. He could certainly spin them, and he often had me crying with laughter.

I think he was with us for five days before he moved on. We were all sorry to see him leave, his humour having provided that little bit of magic. His tragic death a few months later caused great despondency to all who knew and loved him. He was one of life's characters and a true railwayman.

All appeared to be in order, and George's departure heralded the arrival of the auditor. He proved to be a quiet and pleasant man, who missed nothing. The books were examined in detail, then he queried certain blank card ticket stubs in his possession. Happily no serious errors arose, and he went away contented. Auditors were human after all, and not the ogres often portrayed. He would return during the coming months, periodical checks being part of his repertoire. You soon realised that the railway was a mammoth of organisational skill, diverse and complex. One wonders how many other industries could match the complexities of the everyday running of British Railways.

Sadly every complex machine is subject to the occasional breakdown, usually through human error. Tragically this often results in loss of life, and the end of 1963 saw a major crash at Winsford, involving an express passenger train. Just before midnight on Boxing Day the phone rang and Martin informed me of the situation. He had been on duty for more than 12 hours but, as no relief was available, he had no choice but to remain on duty. He urgently requested some hot food and I swiftly cycled to the station to meet his needs and provide some relief. My arrival brought no fresh news and we sat around staring at the telephone. After an hour I returned home, as there was little I could do until the line was cleared.

As I made my way home through the deserted streets, I thought about the casualties; for many this Christmas would be their last. Numerous people were involved in the rescue, and it could hardly be described as a Merry Christmas. Railwaymen are always quick to respond to any tragedy and aware of the dangers railway travel presents. Today's high-speed trains demand intense concentration, and although we have progressed the human factor will sadly always remain.

8
PUPPY LOVE

Entering the booking office one morning I found Martin
peering into a large tea chest. I was invited to look inside and
discovered a small poodle pup, with large sad eyes. Martin was
anxious about the pup's welfare, so had decided to remove it
from its conveyance and give it a meal and a drink. Since the
dog was to be called for, the immediate problem was to contact
the owners and advise them of the pup's arrival. Receiving no
reply, we took the animal to the mess room where it received a
drink. It was obviously hungry so Martin started cooking some
bacon and toast for his and the pup's breakfast. This resulted
in some great tail-wagging and a sly wee on the floor. The little
dog was delighted with his new friends, but as we had work
to do he was quickly returned to his tea chest, whereupon
he fell fast asleep. We eventually contacted the owners, who
immediately collected the dog. While in our care he had eaten
toast, bacon and a KitKat and was still asleep on collection. The
new owners thanked us for our consideration, being delighted
with their purchase.

Occasionally both my parents would be away, resulting in
me looking after our Cairn terrier. 'Scot' was a real character
with a nosey and mischievous nature, and I soon found myself
walking him to work. On arrival he would sit on the booking
office counter studying the passengers. Soon he became a real
personality and, when absent, enquiries were often raised as to
his welfare. At John's instigation Scot was awarded a tail lamp, as
he had become one of the staff. The dog never caused a single
complaint and was always well behaved, which is more than can
be said for the rest of the staff.

It was rare to see a dog at stations as it was against
regulations, but I know of one porter who went everywhere
with his large black dog, the pair being inseparable. Neither

came to any harm during his employment and they often visited various resorts on his days off.

I remember once being accosted by some agitated schoolboys who had spotted an injured dog to the north of the station. I hastily telephoned the RSPCA and they quickly searched for the animal. It was swiftly found, having concussion and a broken leg. Not many dogs survived being hit by a train, but this dog had been lucky and help was at hand. The schoolboys later returned to enquire as to the morning's events, and went away contented. They had saved an animal's life, and the dog would live to see another day.

One of the jobs the porters hated was that of burying cats that had run out of their nine lives. They were constantly crossing the line, resulting in this not infrequent chore. Dogs on the whole fared better, but sometimes met their maker when badly frightened. They would try to outrun an approaching train, which must have been unnerving for any driver. I have, on rare occasions, seen a dog nonchalantly walking between the rails, as if following a path. I must emphasise that walking down a railway line or crossing it can be fraught with danger, and so very nearly cost me my life.

Jimmy Fulton suddenly had the bright idea of creating a football team using the combined staff of the two stations. This was a somewhat difficult task as our combined strength was fewer than 11, so reinforcements were sought with some urgency. This was of even greater necessity on match days, as most of the players were on duty. For some reason I was made captain, and the name of Metropolis United was conceived for our motley team. Subsequent Sundays found several team members kicking hell out of each other during five-a-side games, popularly termed 'friendlies'. As stated, player availability was always a problem, especially when the pubs opened. It was a pity that we didn't have a larger staff, as the railway had a few teams of note, but it is doubtful if we would have been one of them.

British Railways had a staff suggestion scheme that was open to all employees, and it was not long before I participated.

With winter's arrival and the first snow, I watched the porters struggle to remove it from the platforms. My mind conjured up a snowplough that was mobile, and adjustable. Would it be feasible to fit two ploughs to the sides of a brake van, I wondered. They could be spring-loaded to cater for varying platform heights, and swung out and retracted once the snow was cleared. I thought my idea ingenious; however, the suggestion committee thought otherwise, and I received a letter to that effect. It stated their reasons for rejection, but also thanked me for the thought put into the proposal. The main stumbling block was cost, and the fact that the ploughs might foul the running lines. Undeterred, I soon found myself submitting other ideas, which were also unsuccessful, but always acknowledged.

For a short spell we had a influx of pigeon traffic consigned by an eager young man who had high hopes for his flock. Chester was their first destination, and on arrival they would be released, the porter entering on the label (if he remembered) the time and date that this took place. Later these birds travelled to Shrewsbury and we watched their progress with interest. Anyone who has handled pigeons will tell you that they are exceedingly noisy, therefore they were kept of the platform until the train arrived. Then the guard would have to suffer their constant chatter, and the comments from certain guards cannot be repeated. Like most Irishmen, Martin had a keen sense of humour, and thought of a prank to play on our young pigeon-fancier. After the Chester train's departure, Martin explained that instead of putting the pigeons on the train, he had left them in the waiting room. He would release them half an hour after the train's arrival, thus creating a new record for a flight of racing pigeons. However, this event never took place; I managed to talk him out of it, and the pigeons were dispatched on the next train. Even Martin had to concede that pigeons could not fly at 60mph.

I am sure that 1963 saw the introduction of five-day tickets. Prior to their arrival, passengers purchased special cheap day returns, which were extremely popular, accounting for 70 per

The passenger guard

The romance of the guard? Well, think for a while;
I handle the public sometimes fickle and wild;
From drunks to fare-dodgers, old ladies with dogs,
Mischievous schoolboys who leave me their frogs,
Immigrant families and some foreign guests
Who speak little English – if can be a test.
Practical jokers and wild football fans,
I wish that the railway continued their bans.
Tramps with no money, people who are ill –
Sometimes I feel like taking a pill.
Complaints from the public – oh, for some praise!
Often I have 'one of those days'.
Oh the romance of the guard! Well, just think again,
And try to behave when you get on my train!

Barry Allen

cent of our sales. The new tickets were purchased on a Monday
and used for the remainder of the week. Unsurprisingly they
cost more, and we lost our competitive edge, many customers
returning to the buses. Special cheap day returns could only be
purchased after 9.30am, and we lost a lot of goodwill as a result.
Refunds were another problem, resulting in a high number of
claims. It was soon apparent that they were not a success, and
common sense eventually prevailed.

For a small station we sold a lot of London returns, mainly
to the business community. Our season ticket sales were
disappointing, presumably due to the cheapness of special cheap
day returns. Popular day return destinations were Liverpool,
Runcorn, Hartford and Chester. We also handled quite a few
railway warrants, either Forces or Maritime Marine.

I also issued paper tickets and, when necessary, Zone
tickets (for the conveyance of dogs and bicycles). Railway
employees and their families were entitled to privilege travel,

at a reduced rate, such tickets being issued on production of a written request form. For some reason we had to stamp a 'W' on privileged tickets issued to the opposite sex, and I wondered why. Finally there were the ex-Liverpool Lime Street blank card tickets. Passengers did not like queuing at Lime Street, so purchasing their tickets locally saved a lot of hassle.

Internal mail naturally arrived by train, inside a reusable envelope. This envelope was unique. Headed 'Name or Title', 'Department' and 'Station', it could be reused at least 15 times. All sorts of correspondence arose, from job vacancies to training correspondence. If you were lucky, you might receive from Derby a list of surplus items. These could range from barrows, bicycles, name boards and other items. I recall looking at a list of locomotive nameplates. Unfortunately I could not afford one, as my take-home pay for 1963 was £297 0s 19d, after tax. How times have changed!

At Christmas I was often presented with packets of cigarettes by the regular passengers. Embassy, Piccadilly or Woodbine brands were often passed my way, but as I didn't smoke they were passed to the porters. This was to change, as I was now starting to go with the fairer sex and, as they frequently smoked, I joined the club. The porters were no doubt unhappy, as the festive period now rendered little in the way of tips.

Annoyingly all through my stay at West Allerton and later Mossley Hill, we suffered from unannounced platform alterations. The signalman at Speke Junction repeatedly forgot to inform us when he had switched a Liverpool train to Platform 4. This should have been implemented by the ringing of four bells, but it was often unforthcoming. Passengers, seeing that their train was about to arrive on the down slow, would dash across the line, risking life and limb. Other passengers correctly used the footbridge, delaying the train considerably, thus many minutes were lost through this irritating practice.

An unexpected visitor proved to be a British Railways publicity officer, who kept a keen eye on all advertising boards. As we had several, he would select posters for display, ensuring that the porters pasted them up. Special excursions featured heavily in his programme, with a smattering of the more appealing posters showing London or York, etc. I confess that he was good at his job and he visited us quite regularly, much to the dismay of the porters, who disliked this constant attention.

One day Johnny Wakeham suddenly appeared with a bundle of wire wool, required for cleaning Mossley Hill station's metal cladding, which in my opinion would have required an enormous amount of time and effort. Being exempt from the task, he had magically found the necessary material in our stores, and was preparing to send it on the next train. Astonished that such a request had been issued, I telephoned Mossley Hill to find that the instruction had come from Lime Street Chambers. The porters at Mossley Hill, whose supplies had mysteriously vanished, were naturally far from delighted that John had come up with the goods, and soon the line was buzzing with unrepeatable threats. In truth it was an impossible task, and I was astonished that such a request had been issued.

The Station Master suddenly had the whim to publicise our improved train services, which after their initial teething troubles had greatly improved. After all, if you are going to spend millions of pounds electrifying the line, why not get the maximum use out of it? This motivated a large quantity of timetables for distribution to the houses in the surrounding area, and Martin enquired if this included the houses near the pub. He then volunteered for the job, providing he could borrow the Station Master's bicycle. Off he went in the direction of the pub clutching a bundle of timetables, returning an hour later looking tired and glum. He claimed to have delivered several timetables before having a rather unfortunate encounter with a ferocious dog, which had chased him up the road and into the pub. What rotten luck! Later he admitted that he had got fed up delivering individual timetables, shoving four or five through each letterbox in case they had big families. The remainder he had left in the pub. Still, our business did pick up after Martin's efforts, so this time he was ordered to canvass the area in the opposite direction. After all, the Station Master didn't want Martin to meet that wicked dog again…

Safety featured heavily in British Railways' propaganda. Due to the initial mortality of footplate crews and others associated with overhead electrification, I was told to attend the cinema coach at Allerton Diesel Depot. As one might expect, the films showed cause and effect, and correct working practices. Electrification had created many widows, especially among firemen who still climbed on tenders to bring the coal forward. Old habits die hard, and there were many such casualties in our high-speed age.

9
WHAT A RELIEF

It was normal practice, when any porter was absent through illness or holidays, for a relief man to be sent. David Richardson and Tony Matthews covered absenteeism on more than one occasion, and were unforgettable characters. Tony was a fanatical Evertonian, and as I supported Liverpool one can imagine the banter that ensued. In truth both teams were highly successful, but to a Scouser you had only one allegiance, depended on your upbringing. Tony, however, was comparatively quiet compared to Dave Richardson, who was a born comedian. This gentleman soon got up to some pranks that made the Station Master's hair curl.

I will never forget his fire bucket escape. Due to frost damage the toilet was out of order and following a number of complaints Dave had a brainwave. Hanging in the booking office corridor were a string of fire buckets containing sand, so he hung a toilet roll over each bucket, just in case nature urgently called, and it nearly did when the Station Master saw them.

On another occasion, finding himself locked out of the booking office, Dave decided to climb the waste pipe to gain access to the mess room. Unaware of his actions until I heard the shouts, I looked out of the window to find him hanging from the waste pipe, it having detached itself from the wall and split, showering him with its contents. He was covered from head to foot in tealeaves. I could not move as I was crying with laughter. Meanwhile Dave was uttering loud curses and groans as the pipe came further away from the wall, lowering him at an increasing speed towards some blackberry bushes. Having landed with a shriek, he proceeded to make his way up to the booking office. On entering, he immediately began to sing an Al Jolson number, such was his sense of humour.

One of the things that brought great delight to all and

sundry was the writing on the toilet walls. Mossley Hill boasted a far better vocabulary, all of us agreeing that this was the influence of the students from the nearby university. John would scrub off the graffiti, but it quickly reappeared after his efforts and it seemed a rather pointless task. Another of John's dislikes was painting the platform edges with white lime, a practice that seems to have fallen by the wayside these days. When Martin attempted this, he always managed to get more lime on his uniform than on the platform edge. John, however, was the appointed expert and did a grand job, even if he did hate doing it. Once done, he would stand back and admire his work, having completed four platforms with consummate skill.

Mr Squires had moved on some months previously, being replaced by various relief Station Masters, including Mr Turner, one of the old guard, who was both knowledgeable and experienced, and longing for retirement. I began to wonder if they would ever fill the vacancy, as various Station Masters came and went.

I had worked at Mossley Hill on several occasions covering absenteeism and holidays, and all had gone smoothly so far, One morning I had a real shock when I was in the middle of booking the 10.29am for Chester. I was unexpectedly confronted by a Scout Master who asked for one and 26 halves for Chester! Completely speechless, I asked why he had not notified us in advance. He had, but nobody had passed the message on. Thank goodness for paper tickets! These were a means whereby I could write a single ticket covering the entire party. The ticket collectors at Chester would no doubt love me, but it was quicker than issuing 26 halves. It was swiftly done and, having received a cheque, I breathed a sigh of relief. The group sauntered past, containing several mischievous-looking characters, and headed for the ramp. This was a popular train and normally packed. I wondered if they would all get on. Once the train left I rechecked my calculations, finding them correct. What a relief – no calculators in those days, just chalk, a desktop and, if you were lucky, a ready reckoner.

Back at West Allerton things were changing rapidly. Martin,

having taken a signalling correspondence course, decided to become a shunter at Edge Hill, an extremely illogical move. I was sorry to see him go, as we had both done the course together. I found it extremely interesting, and a lot of the problems really made you think. Sadly modernisation was erasing many of the smaller signal boxes and there seemed no future in it.

John Wakeham remained with me for the time being, although he was pondering a move back to Mossley Hill, or threatening to leave the railway for a job with better pay, a familiar tale. Eddie Randles, Martin's replacement, I had already encountered, as

Porter Eddie Randles poses outside the Wymans book stall at West Allerton in 1964. *Author's collection*

he used to chase me off the platform at Garston station. He did not like trainspotters.

I was soon to learn that he had a passion for cleaning floors and windows. Woe betide anyone who stepped on his handiwork. Eddie had considerable experience, having served at several stations, including Mossley Hill, before his move to West Allerton. Rather small and rotund, Eddie had been nicknamed 'Wagon Wheels' by the railway fraternity – how and why I never found out. He was in his late 50s and not afraid of doing his share. Thankfully he possessed a sense of humour, and enjoyed a good prank, provided it was not played on him.

Not to be outdone by our Cheshire Lines rivals, I decided to have a go at winning the station garden prize. Finding some old bricks, I spent a couple of mornings making three small flower beds and painting them with white gloss – they looked a treat. My enthusiasm swiftly rubbed off on John, and in a moment of madness he dug up the bank behind Platform 1, tipping the soil on the platform. This act did not please Divisional Manager Mr Cochran who, on seeing the deposit, telephoned the acting Station Master and told him to remove it post-haste. This was no sooner said than done, but it did knock some the heart out of John, who had grand ideas for the embankment. July brought its reward, the asters, stocks and snapdragons looking particularly striking among the marigolds and lobelias. Sadly we did not win a prize or commendation, but we had tried, and felt quite proud of our efforts.

All the station staff where very friendly with Mrs Mason, the lady in charge of the Wymans kiosk, and I soon found myself dating her pretty daughter. John nicknamed Mrs Mason 'Maceface', and this was the name she was stuck with during my period at West Allerton. On occasions respectable-looking gentlemen would sneak in to buy *Playboy* magazine. It was great fun seeing their faces as they turned round only to find us standing behind them, John having all these patrons well taped.

Two people who called in on a daily basis where John Boyd and Albert Connell. Attached to Wavertree Parcels Depot, their Thames van would appear like a homing pigeon just as we were frying a bacon sandwich. Curses would be uttered, as our bacon sandwiches were popular in the extreme. We even tried changing our break times, but it made no difference. The pair would enter grinning like Cheshire cats, making straight for the kitchen. They did have a legitimate reason for visiting the station, but it did not include drinking our tea and eating our sandwiches. Nevertheless, they were always made welcome, receiving a considerable amount of leg-pulling and always gave as good as they got. Later Albert became our new porter, greatly increasing his wages.

Eddie Haley, another British Railways driver, arrived daily on his BSA Gold Star 500cc motorcycle, noisily revving it up to impress the neighbours. His bike incorporated many accessories, the only thing missing being an outside loo; and once you had been a pillion passenger, you generally needed one. Eddie worked for the Runcorn Goods Department, making his living driving a Scammell 'mechanical horse' on local deliveries. These three-wheeled vehicles were not exactly speedy, but they had gained an excellent reputation for turning in tight spaces, having replaced the traditional horse-drawn dray. Goods work certainly had its benefits – life was much more sedate, and you never rushed. We became good friends and later, after I had left the railway, I attended Eddie's wedding. Sadly Runcorn Goods is no more, nor are the mechanical horses a familiar scene, such is the changing face of our modern railway.

If you were lucky, the station would be subjected to a major clean, a task normally performed by a gang of women cleaners accompanied by a supervisor. They would sing merrily away, working efficiently down each platform removing years of grime. Once they had finished, the station sparkled and the painters would arrive. After they had completed their task, you had a station to be proud of. We felt like the owner of a new house, eyeing it up continuously until the novelty wore off.

An unusual incident occurred one evening when John was walking between the two stations – not recommended, whatever the circumstances. Strolling down the slow line, he was suddenly showered with parcels from a passing train. Completely surprised, John tried his best to retrieve them, but it proved impossible due to the quantity involved. Carrying various parcels, he made his way to West Allerton and immediately telephoned the signalman at Speke Junction, requesting that he stop and examine the offending train. Unfortunately the train had long passed and the signalman suggested to John that he contact the British Transport Police. Having done so, John then went back to retrieve more parcels. Having established that the train was secure, the police took the matter in hand. Clearly suspicious, they settled down to wait, and John had to cease his rescue efforts. Shortly after midnight a small van pulled up and a figure scrambled down the bank. The police pounced and arrested the train guard and his accomplice. The guard had made a costly mistake, as he had not expected anyone to be in the vicinity.

Railway widows came in all shapes and sizes, and Mrs Edge became a regular visitor, travelling into the city to visit the shops or see friends. Her husband had lost his life at Edge Hill, adding another statistic to the numerous engine drivers killed by unseen locomotives. During my railway career I met many widows, and I can honestly say they were seldom merry, often struggling to survive on a state or railway pension. Loneliness is a curse, and for many life lost its purpose once their partners had gone.

Many unions operated within British Railways. Having been encouraged to join the Transport Salaried Staffs' Association (TSSA), the clerical workers' union, I found myself somewhat isolated, as certain of my colleagues had joined the National Union of Railwaymen (NUR), thinking it a more aggressive union. Most of the hourly-paid belonged to the NUR, but there was a certain reluctance to get involved in protests or strikes. This was soon to change, as Doctor Beeching lurked around the corner and our jobs seemed suddenly vulnerable. The atmosphere was changing to one of disenchantment. Many experienced staff where departing and our railway would never be quite the same again. I began to feel restless.

10
I MOVE TO MOSSLEY HILL

If my memory serves me correctly John Wakeham eventually found a more lucrative position elsewhere. I was sorry to see him go, and he was replaced by Albert Connell, whose posting I touched on previously. Albert possessed a unique talent: he was a brilliant cartoonist, and could draw an 'Andy Capp' caption in the blink of an eye. It was a shame that his ability remained unrecognised.

Alan Chesworth, Mossley Hill's young booking clerk, was keen to rid himself of shift work, as it interfered with his courting arrangements resulting in a request to swap duties. I felt that a move would be in my interests, having been at West Allerton for more than two years, so I readily agreed. This caused some despondency among the porters (we were a two-faced lot) and in many respects I was sorry to go. Any regrets swiftly vanished once I found myself standing in Mossley Hill's booking office, not exactly strange territory. I swiftly familiarised myself with the new ticket rack, wondering what fresh challenges lay ahead.

Mossley Hill station had been completely rebuilt under the Liverpool to London modernisation programme. Nothing of the old station survived, except for the closed goods yard. At one time a 'Super D' locomotive could be found shunting wagons in the thriving coal yard, but this had long gone. One of the sidings was still used for empty stock, and normally hosted a string of old carriages. Typical of most structures erected during the upheaval, it lacked atmosphere. I could not help thinking about the old building, with its enclosed wooden ramps. The waiting rooms were always welcoming, radiating the heat of coal fires. Now we had electric fires, which seldom worked, even after repair. The brasswork and flower beds had also disappeared, and the building seemed dull and impersonal. I never took to this new breed of railway structure, much preferring what had gone before. It had two short platforms serving the up and down fast and up and down slow lines. Not much to get excited about, but such is progress!

On my arrival the station had a new Station Master, who hailed from Scotland, and I have a feeling his name was Thompson. He immediately received a forged memo from the Passenger Manager's office, stating that he was only allowed to wear his kilt on the Queen's Birthday. Nicknamed 'Jock', we soon found that he possessed a sharp mind, and was a good organiser.

The porters included 'Taffy' Williams, who left shortly after my arrival to take up a position with the overhead maintenance department, and Eddie Gasgoine, who was later joined by his son. Unfortunately he was blessed with the same Christian name, causing endless confusion. The clerks were Jimmy Fulton and yours truly. West Allerton's porters covered for any absenteeism, and it was not unusual for me to be working with one of my old colleagues.

One of my duties was compiling wages for the staff at both locations. This was a new experience for me and not without its moments. When working out overtime it was not unusual to have a porter breathing down your neck, to see what he was about to pick up. I recall walking in one afternoon to be greeted with hoots of derision (I'm being polite) from Jimmy Fulton, who promptly called me a so and so for wrongly compiling the wages. I was astonished until he pointed out that I had forgotten to include the new pay award, leaving an energetic Mr Fulton to sort out the mess. I pointed out that anyone could make a mistake, and I was only human. On that point, the Station Master and James Fulton disagreed.

Another job was that of compiling the wages for Ditton Creosote Works. The money arrived by armed guard and, after it had been carefully counted, it was sealed within a leather pouch and carried down to the Chester train. Then the guard would sign for the pouch and throw it in the brake van – mind-boggling, considering that the pouch contain a few thousand

The old Mossley Hill goods

For years I watched the daily goods train
Pulled by an old 'Super D'
Wheezing along with her squealing load
To delight a youth such as me.
She would plod off the slow and into the yard,
Then reverse and drop off the brake.
A brief conversation between shunter and guard
To decide what action to take.
The shunter seemed fit as he raced up and down
Whilst organised chaos took a hold;
He would pin down a brake and then, with a frown,
Watch the wagon continue to roll.
With a great thumping crash, buffers would clash,
And coal dust would fly through the air,
While the shunter continued to make a terrible hash
And at the footplate crew constantly glare.
The guard would be watching and shaking his head
Whilst the footplate crew grinned with great glee,
As the shunter tripped and then had a good swear
To delight a youth such as me…

Barry Allen

pounds. Sadly Ditton Creosote Works, together with the cash bag, have faded into oblivion, and we were never robbed, another of life's fairy stories.

I was now on regular shifts, working early and late turn on a fortnightly basis. I was also required to work Sunday mornings once a fortnight, not exactly a thrilling prospect. Mind you, as a railwayman you had to expect weekend work, and you simply got on with it. By now I had become accustomed to my new position, and things had become routine.

The football season was once more upon us, with the usual Saturday specials. Thankfully our involvement was minimal, football specials having a fearsome reputation. Imagine, then, our dismay on receiving word that we would host a football special carrying Everton fans from an FA Cup game at Wolverhampton. Management's decision to stop the train at Allerton and Mossley Hill took us completely by surprise. The arrival of the Station Master on his day off meant that something was afoot, and he swiftly explained his plans for dealing with the train. This included putting a barrow across the exit, a quick course in unarmed combat and the issuing of a BR prayer book. The barrow seemed a good idea, as it only allowed one person through at a time. I was to be the lucky one, collecting the tickets at the barrier, while Albert supported me. The Station Master would have a roving role dealing with any emergency.

To say that the train was running late is an understatement. At last a phone call from Allerton confirmed our worst fears – it was on its way. They had experienced trouble and were happy to see it depart. After a couple of visits to the toilet I was ready. On hearing that Everton had drawn, the Station Master thought that the supporters would be reasonably happy; however, I remained unconvinced. The train eventually arrived on the slow line, hauled by a wheezing 'Black Five'. I watched as the doors flew open, discharging a mass of fans, most marching towards me in an orderly fashion. Soon I was collecting tickets and everything seemed to be going according to plan, so Albert left me to try and shut the carriage doors. Certain carriages seemed to be in chaos; no sooner had a door been shut than it would fly open again. This was due to certain drunken youths acting stupidly. A couple of railway policemen and their dogs were patrolling the train, but seemed unable to control the situation, probably because they were simply short-handed.

After the initial rush approximately 20 fans stood on the platform gazing in my direction, and I began to feel apprehensive. Shouting 'Charge!' they rushed towards me as the Station Master frantically blew his whistle. I stood my ground, but finished up on my back, tickets being shoved in my top pocket, stuffed down my neck or thrown on top of me. Like lightning the group disappeared, only half of them having possessed tickets. I struggled to my feet and, since there was little I could do, I went to assist in getting the train away. Stupidity still prevailed and a bottle came hurling out of the train, just missing the Station Master. I started to shut the carriage doors and was immediately grabbed by the lapels in an effort to steal the tickets sticking out of my top pocket. Totally dejected, the engine driver watched our performance with indifference. When I finally engaged him in conversation, all he could say was 'Bring back hanging, and that so-and-so communication cord'. Not amused by my joke about him getting a Sunday out of it, the train finally left, puffing away towards Lime Street, a defiant toot signifying the last lap.

This was the only football special I ever dealt with, these trains being the brunt of many a joke by Jimmy Tarbuck. The railway eventually wised up and the trains were banned, which must have come as a great relief all round.

The arrival of winter usually heralded snow and ice, which for safety reasons had to be removed from the platforms. I recall a particular Sunday when it snowed continuously; once it had ceased I started clearing it from the two long ramps leading to the platforms (which in earlier LNWR days had been covered), consuming a considerable amount of energy in the process. No sooner had I stood back to admire my handiwork than it started to snow again, leading to a few choice expletives. I should add that this task was normally performed by the porter, but on this occasion he had not turned in, and I was awaiting a replacement. As you can guess, we went through a lot of salt keeping the platforms clear during the winter months.

Given the opportunity, Albert and I would proceed to Edge Hill after finishing an early shift to play football with the goods guards waiting to sign on. Anyone could join in these games, and often did. They were scrappy affairs, and on one occasion a dog ran off with our ball, a string of swear words echoing in its wake. The dog then let us approach, and just when we thought we had the ball, it would run off with it, having great fun. Thus we were minus a ball for quite some considerable time. On another occasion I was introduced to a tough-looking character, recently released from Walton Prison for GBH. Albert commented, 'Don't worry, he's on our side.' This gentleman went on to score a hat trick due to some reluctant tackles from the opposition. What wonderful days they were, and we probably put as much effort into these games as was required to fire a steam engine. As for the guards, they usually lost.

Two of our regular commuters were a rather attractive pair of identical twin girls who often travelled into Liverpool Lime Street. One evening I was travelling to Lime Street and happened to find myself opposite one of them. Immediately I sat beside her and it was not long before I had made a date. Naturally I was feeling quite pleased with myself, and we went out for quite a while. I could never tell them apart, as they dressed similarly, with matching hairstyles. Indeed, their mother struggled at times to distinguish them, especially at mealtimes.

One night we were strolling along when I realised that I was receiving some quite vague answers when discussing recent events. Suddenly the penny dropped – I was out with the other twin! She confessed that they both took great delight in swapping boyfriends and comparing experiences. I was somewhat shocked, and felt a bit of a fool. Needless to say, our relationship soon ended, as I never knew who I was out with. To the twins this was a constant source of amusement, and they were probably well practised in this art.

I had a miraculous escape while working one wet Saturday night. Due to a porter's absence and no relief being available, the Station Master requested that I carry out his duties for the night, finishing once the last train had departed at approximately 11.20pm. Having agreed, I found myself trudging down the ramp shortly before the arrival of the 10.47pm to Crewe, heralding a brief spell of activity, as the 10.50 to Holyhead would be along shortly after. The Crewe was scheduled for the slow, and it was on the slow platform that I found myself sheltering from the pouring rain, accompanied by a few disgruntled passengers. The train arrived behind a brand-new electric locomotive, and soon I was engaging the guard in conversation, only to hear the sound of an approaching train.

'Aye up, here's the Holyhead,' called the guard, and turning I saw that train entering the station on the fast line, hauled by a 'Black Five' locomotive. The engine immediately started to blow off, creating an awful din. Without further delay I gave the guard the tip and began running to the rear of the train, in an effort to reach the fast platform. I had just jumped onto the track, seeking the Holyhead's guard, when an electric-hauled express flashed by on the down fast, missing me by about 2 feet. Instinctively I threw myself backwards, dropping my hand lamp, and landed with a thud on the slow line, banging my head and legs.

Completely shaken, I staggered to my feet only to see the guard of the Holyhead train running towards me in a highly agitated state. On reaching me he called me 'a bloody fool', then quietly asked me if I was all right. He had anticipated my actions and had been trying to warn me of the approaching train. In truth, I was far from all right, as I was shaking violently, so he suggested that I send for relief to cover the remainder of my duties. Knowing that nobody else was available, I decided to stick it out. Still fussing, the guard repeated his advice; however, he was interrupted by a few sharp blasts from the engine's whistle, as the driver, unaware of what had transpired, was anxious to be away. Suddenly the engine ceased blowing off and silence returned to the station. To avoid any more hold-ups I soon got the train away, after promising the guard that I would make myself a cup of tea and have a rest. While walking painfully towards the booking office, I reflected on my narrow escape, having missed death by seconds. I had been a very lucky lad indeed. The guard had been right to call me a bloody fool, only this time I had lived to tell the tale. Other poor souls, having made similar mistakes, had not.

On a Sunday night the equivalent of the 'Merseyside Express' stopped at Mossley Hill, en route to Liverpool Lime Street, being the only London express to do so. A few years earlier the 'Shamrock' had stopped here daily, together with the returning 'Merseyside Express'. However, with modernisation came changes, namely the loss of these trains to Runcorn. They were no longer titled expresses, and some of the romance disappeared with electrification.

Due to similar circumstances to those mentioned above, I once again found myself doing the porter's duties, the station having been hit by a flu epidemic. A few weeks had passed since my narrow escape and I tentatively awaited the arrival of the London train, thinking it something of an accolade to be dealing with one of these expresses. It arrived on time, hauled by an electric locomotive pulling 11 carriages. Due to the shortness of the platforms it was necessary for the train to draw up, allowing passengers to leave the train. I gave the guard the correct signal, and the train drew forward. Once achieved, I gave the guard the 'right away' signal consisting of a white light, not a green, which is the popular belief. The guard then gave me a green, which I in turn passed to the driver and the train departed. This had been a novel experience and one that I thoroughly enjoyed. Sadly it was never to be repeated, as I was to leave the railway within a few months. By now the 'Beeching Plan' was in full swing, and my aspirations were disappearing quicker than the rural branch lines.

The great puzzle for myself, and many others, was relatively simple. Why pay a man, in this case Doctor Beeching, who knew nothing of railways, £24,000 a year to close lines? If he had thought of a way to make threatened railway lines pay, then surely the good Doctor would have been worth his colossal salary. In truth the people who ran British Railways, i.e. the employees, were never asked for their ideas. Knowing the experience that existed within its ranks, I would suggest that had such an exercise been carried out the results would have been surprising.

By the spring of 1965 rumours of local closure were rife, these having an unsettling effect on me and the rest of the staff. At this time I was courting, and money was being more passionately sought than in previous years. The railway was changing, and modernisation meant fewer jobs, therefore I started to seek other employment. It was a momentous decision, but one I have seldom regretted. Within weeks I obtained a new position, leading to me handing in my notice in the late spring.

A lot of the people mentioned in this book have sadly died, including Albert, who met an untimely death in Blackpool. Eddie Randles and my Uncle Jim have also passed away; the latter caused me particular distress, having accompanied him to many preserved lines in the north of England. I would like to add that my school pal Phil Ebsworth's BR career blossomed, working his way through the ranks to hold a senior management position in the London area.

I thank my former workmates for some wonderful memories, thus providing me with the inspiration to write this book.

11
JAMES STONE: BRUNSWICK DRIVER AND RAILWAY PHOTOGRAPHER

Before completing this book with memories of some of railwayman I have known, I would like to turn the clock back to pre-war days.

Jimmy Stone joined the cleaning staff at Brunswick shed in the early 1930s, working his way up through the ranks to become a driver after spending years firing many of the former GCR classes still active on the CLC.

Reputedly an excellent driver, his passion for photography is clearly demonstrated. Taken with his new Voigtlander camera, his pictures offer a rare glimpse of the various classes to be found on the CLC in the Liverpool area shortly before and after the Second World War.

All the photographs were taken in the area around Mersey Road station and the adjacent Otterspool Loop, approximately 2 miles east of Brunswick, a stretch of line rarely visited by enthusiasts. The Cheshire Lines were never enthusiastically embraced by railway photographers; many, like Eric Treacy, confined their activities to the Edge Hill area.

I would imagine that Jimmy had prior knowledge of any special workings, many of his subjects having been specially selected. With the passing of time, all records have been lost and any information regarding these specials would be most welcome.

Interestingly, Mersey Road station still survives, having closed and reopened, and is now part of the Merseyrail electric system. The loop at Otterspool has long since returned to nature, still hidden by a high embankment, and Otterspool signal box is just a memory. I still recall seeing a 4F impatiently awaiting release from the loop during a visit to Otterspool box in 1960.

Jimmy never lost his love of steam or photography, and after the war he returned to his favourite location to photograph BR steam.

For an engine driver to record such images is unusual, and he must have endured some ribbing from his footplate colleagues. Having experienced retired Brunswick drivers at play, comments bounce off them like water off a duck's back, and Jimmy would have taken such repartee in his stride.

I would like to take this opportunity to thank his son Malcolm, who kept up the family tradition, for bringing these fascinating photographs to light. All the pictures appear by courtesy of the Gordon Coltas Trust.

In 1938 ex-GCR '800 Class' (LNER Class 'D6') No 5871 passes through Mersey Road with a Manchester to Liverpool express. During the Second World War these locos often had their safety valves wedged closed before departing with a heavy train.

In 1938 the crew of 'N5' No 5911 appears to include a station master, who is standing just behind the young fireman. The loco is probably returning from Halewood Siding, where it would have been put to good use.

An up Liverpool to Manchester express passes through Mersey Road in 1938 behind 'D9' No 5111. These were very capable engines and handled the majority of the inter-city workings.

This second view of a 'D9', No 6020, provides a closer view of Mersey Road station.

A good servant of the CLC was the handsome 'D9' Class of 4-4-0s. No 6028 is seen here trundling through Mersey Road with an express. Brunswick shed had a good number of these popular machines.

'J39' Standard Goods No 1272 passes through on the down main with what appears to be a special working. The first carriage is of interest, and the train is carrying express passenger headlamps.

Ex-GCR 'D11' 'Director' Class No 5511 *Mons* is on a Hull train.

Kitson-built 'Q4' 0-8-0 No 6175 trundles through the station towards
Manchester with a mixed freight. The front portion appears to be
vacuum-fitted.

This very rare photo shows 'V2' 2-6-2 No 4828 passing through Mersey
Road en route to Liverpool Central with a Sheffield working just before
the war. These locos were swiftly banned from Liverpool Central
because of a mishap on the turntable at Brunswick when a fireman was
badly crushed.

Here's another rare view of 'B17' 'Footballer' No 2864 *Liverpool* speeding towards Garston and about to pass Liverpool Cricket Club with a Harwich train in 1938.

Large-boilered 2-6-2T No 40203 leaves Mersey Road with a local for Liverpool Central in 1959, viewed from Otterspool signal box.

A Stanier 2-6-4T is seen at Mersey Road station on a Manchester to Liverpool express in about 1961. These engines were ideally suited to this task.

LNER Class 'B9' ex-Great Central Railway 4-6-0 'Baby Fish' Class, on the up line at Mersey Road in 1939.

Ex-Great Northern Railway 'C1' Class 4-4-2 No 3287 with a down Hull to Liverpool Central service. Note the fish vans at the front of the train.

An extract from the BR Timetable map of 1963.

Right: Part of the original 1892 track diagram of Huskisson Dock's goods yard removed from the box around 1941. Both the box and the goods yard were put out of action

when the Brocklebank steamer *SS Malakand*, sister ship *SS Mahout*, and several others were destroyed in the bombing raid of 3/4 May 1941. Note the 'explosion marks' on the diagram. The dock remained largely inoperable for the remainder of the war. *Author's collection*

12
THE GARSTON COFFIN DODGERS

Having covered my career with British Railways, I would now like to take the opportunity to introduce the Garston Coffin Dodgers, a group of retired drivers and firemen who worked at the various Merseyside sheds in the days of steam. Many have since sadly passed away, but the survivors still manage to soldier on, having recently lost their beloved LMS Club to developers.

The Garston Coffin Dodgers: former British Railways staff leave the London Midland Region club in July 2006. Without their input I could not have written their stories. From left to right, they are Tommy Holden, the late Trevor Gargon, the late Harry Grieve, Spencer Wissett, A. C. Jones, the late Ray Helsby, Eddie McDonald, the late Brian Cassidy and the late Pat Mitchell. All but Messrs McDonald and Cassidy were former Brunswick and Speke CLC footplatemen.

They meet every Thursday afternoon at the Swan public house in Garston, Liverpool, the gatherings being noisy and boisterous affairs. Their tales are interesting and factual, providing a fascinating glimpse into life on the footplate during the steam era. Here are some of their stories.

On 2 July 1966 the Cheshire Lines Association put on a special train for the company's former employees, some having worked for the CLC for more than 50 years. The CLC relinquished its independence in 1948 with the birth of British Railways. The train consisted of Ivatt 2-6-0 No 46516 and two carriages, and was scheduled to call at various station on the old Cheshire Lines system. It is seen here standing at Widnes North, crewed by driver Charlie Mapley and my old mate Ray Gosling. Also depicted chatting is solicitor R. K. Warburton, who was well known for his love of railways; indeed, he is reputed to

have had an extensive model railway in his billiard room, together with a collection of railway lamps and signals. Ray describes the day as having been arduous, as their allocated engine failed on shed, making them late; they were therefore chasing their tail all day. It was nonetheless a memorable outing for all concerned, paying tribute to employees who gave a lifetime's service to the former CLC.
Courtesy of Widnes Weekly News

Fortunately a lot of retired or working drivers from Virgin and other privatised companies are now swelling their ranks. They enjoy some excellent outings, superbly organised by Alan Jordan, a former driver and TA Officer. Their main claim to fame was their appearance of ITV's Granada Reports news programme – memorable indeed. Granada covered their initial trip to the Llangollen Railway, and they have also been featured in the local press.

The late Douglas Carver, 8C Speke shed

When working on the Western Region, Douglas and his colleagues were very fond of the '57XX' pannier tanks, running between Worcester, Stratford-upon-Avon and Cheltenham. One day, after completing their normal run, with Douglas firing, they were approached by a very excited individual who was waving a stopwatch and a sheet of paper.

'You did 85mph back there!' he exclaimed, and ran back to the coach for the return journey.

Douglas said that enginemen never really knew the speed of their engines, as they had no speedometers. They only knew the timings between stations, and ran as fast as necessary to maintain schedules. It is interesting that he was also timed again with a '57XX' at 77mph running bunker-first with an eight-coach train. He said that they probably achieved speeds of this nature quite regularly, but left it to the enthusiasts to work out the results. What it must have been like on the footplate defies imagination, as keeping your balance must have been extremely difficult.

The bodies of the early 'Warship' diesel-hydraulics were prone to overheating after long runs, and it was not uncommon for the doors to jam due to expansion. At various stations, including Paddington, this presented a problem. Many drivers had to exit via the cab windows, the doors being firmly shut. This must have been quite embarrassing for all concerned, especially if the driver was portly, as he was well and truly trapped.

Edge Hill fireman and driver Spencer Wissett is at the controls of preserved 'A4' No 60009 *Union of South Africa*. Author's collection

60009

Spencer Wissett, 8A Edge Hill shed

Spencer was firing 'Pacific' No 46208 *Princess Helena Victoria* on a bullion train via Runcorn in the early hours when his driver, Charlie Ebsworth, said, 'Let's see what she will do.'

They swiftly accelerated to 115mph before Charlie closed the regulator. Now Charlie was a known speed merchant and Spencer saw the speedometer touch 115mph. Their load was extremely light, so I asked him how the engine had handled at such a speed. Spencer replied that he was not aware that they were going so fast until Charlie pointed to the speedometer. Like a lot of claims, their speed cannot be verified, but Charlie Ebsworth later told his son that he had touched 115mph when steaming down the bank, and I do not doubt the story.

The late Billy Marriott, 27F Brunswick shed

The following took place at Brunswick shed. The Marriotts were not beyond playing a joke, and our story concerns Bill's father Jack and his Uncle Bill. Boiler washouts were normally performed by Bob Bell; however, another of his duties was clearing ash from the pits. Seeing a large pile of ash, Jack Marriott said to Bob, 'What's that in the ash?' and jumping into the pit he came out with half a crown in his hand. 'Looks like

A youthful driver Bill Marriot (right) and his fireman Dick Manley at Brunswick Shed in the late 1950s.

someone's dropped some money into the ash.'

Bob looked at him suspiciously and muttered, 'Well, that's my ash, now clear off.'

A few minutes later Bill walked past to find Bob peering into the pile. Jumping down he dug into the ash and came up with another half crown. 'Lucky I spotted that, Bob,' he said, tossing it up and down. Bob exploded.

'That's my ash!' he screamed. 'Now you Marriotts clear off.'

Hiding behind an engine, Jack and Bill (senior) watched as Bob descended into the pit and started sieving the ash, completely unaware that Bill and Jack had jumped into the pit with half crowns in their hands. In various states of hysterics, they walked past Bob, tossing their half crowns, when suddenly the penny (or should I say half crown?) dropped, and Bob went mad, being the victim of a typical railway joke. I can assure readers that it was unwise to apply for railway employment unless you could take a joke.

Such occurrences were part of everyday life. Knowing the character involved, I would imagine that it would not take Bob

Bill Marriott in the engine room of a Class 47. *Author's collection*
Gorton 'Crab' 2-6-0 No 42775 is about to pass Brunswick shed.
Author's collection

long to get his own back. After all, one good prank deserves another!

Towards the end of the war, Brunswick shed received an American 'S160' loco for demonstration purposes. After they had inspected her, driver Bert Foulkes and fireman Bill Fletcher were ordered to take her light engine to Northwich. Deciding to oil around, Bert ordered Bill to reverse the engine so he could oil the big ends. Bill duly obliged and, after placing her in reverse gear, opened the regulator. Instantly the engine sped off towards a line of parked engines up against the buffer stops. Bill frantically tried to close the regulator, unaware that it contained a racket that required releasing prior to closure. With an almighty crash the 'S160' thumped into the parked engines, her wheels spinning violently as her exhaust rattled the rafters. By this time Bert had raced from the pit and jumped into the cab to release the regulator. They then left the cab arguing furiously as to who was to blame for the mishap. At this precise moment, years of accumulated soot and ash, having been duly loosened, descended from the shed roof onto the pair, covering them from head to foot. Still arguing, they entered the mess room to peals of laughter. Bill said they looked like a couple of black and white minstrels, and the shed staff were in hysterics.

In 1943 Bill became a passed cleaner, and was booked to fire the 2.30pm train from Liverpool Central to Southport via Manchester. He was surprised to find that 'B17' *West Ham United* had been rostered instead of the usual 'D9'. His mate, Southport driver Albert Bentham, looked apprehensive, having never driven the class before. Soon all nerves disappeared and they were quickly into their stride, taking the sharp curve at Sankey Junction at approximately 35mph. On hitting the curve, the engine cab lifted 2 to 3 inches off the frame before crashing down, terrifying the pair. Arriving at Manchester Central they were confronted by two Gorton men who had been travelling 'on the cushions' in the train. One asked, 'What the hell are you doing with this engine?' – it had been failed by Gorton shed. Unfortunately they were stuck with it for their run to Southport and carefully nursed it to Lord Street, only to find it too long for the turntable. There they left it, returning home via the rival electrified line. Billy never liked Gresley engines, especially 'B17s'.

The late Ray Harrison, 8G Sutton Oak

As a youngster Ray was based at St Helens and one of his regular duties was firing Ivatt Class 2 'Mickey Mouse' tanks on the Skelmersdale to St Helens push-pulls. Ray said they were grand engines with a wonderful turn of speed. One evening they were due to return to St Helens with the shuttle when the driver discovered that he was having trouble with the regulator, the problem relating to the vacuum pump, located alongside the smokebox. One of the traditional ways of dealing with a sticking pump was to hit it with a hammer, thus releasing it. The driver asked Ray if he could stand on the footplate for the return journey and hit the pump at regular intervals so that their passengers could get home for their tea! Ray duly obliged, forgetting that it was a winter's evening and that he was only wearing his thin cotton overalls. Ray clung onto the handrail for dear life and did his stuff as the train reached more than 50mph.

By the time they reached St Helens he was absolutely frozen and was helped off the running plate by his elderly driver, who warmly thanked him for his efforts. The next thing Ray heard was the sound of spontaneous applause. The passengers, having observed Ray's unselfish act, lined up on the platform to express their thanks, a memory he always cherished. I asked him if he would have repeated the exercise, to which he replied, 'Of course – I was a railwayman.' This wonderful story emphasises the commitment of former footplate staff.

The late Harry Grieve, 27F Brunswick

Early in the war the dwindling number of 'D6' locomotives were beginning to show their age. Poor maintenance and heavy loadings providing a real test for crews rostered on these veterans. When faced with getting a heavy train away from Liverpool Central, certain drivers resorted to drastic and potentially dangerous measures to increase boiler pressure. An actuating lever curved from the top of the Ramsbottom safety valves into the front of the cab, entering by way of an elongated hole, just below the whistle. Drivers found that jamming a brush into the hole stopped the movement of the lever, ensuring that the locomotive could not blow off. This was not one for the instruction manual, although it must be stressed that the drivers in question were highly experienced. One can assume that they knew what they were doing, as there is no record of a 'D6' coming to grief. Records show that that these engines sometimes pulled loads in excess of 400 tons. One outstanding performer, No 5853, frequently worked the Hull train, handling it with ease. When drivers resorted to this expedient, Harry quite naturally became very nervous, as he watched the gauge creep over its maximum pressure. Once the train started moving the brush was removed, much to his relief.

A wartime collision involving an ammunition train and light engine occurred at Brunswick, which could have been catastrophic. Shortly before midnight an 'N5' tank arrived with 30 loose-coupled vans full of ammunition, the train having been stabled at Widnes to avoid the attention of enemy bombers. As it entered the loop it started to run away, and the driver urgently popped his whistle to alert the signalman that his train was out of control. Immediately the signalman switched the train back to the main line, giving the driver more time to stop. Unfortunately he had forgotten that a 'K3' was waiting to work the 1.15am Dewsnap Goods. With a loud crash the 'N5' ran into the front of the 'K3', pushing it back approximately 15 yards. Its driver, Harry Simmons, and his fireman, Les Clark, received severe bruising and shock, while the 'N5' sustained only minor damage and no vans were derailed, although the crew somewhat shaken but unhurt. Considerable damage was done to the 'K3', the front end and smokebox bearing the brunt of the impact. Also the front buffers sheared off, and it was fortunate that Les Clark had not applied the hand brake, otherwise the damage could have been far worse. One shudders to think what might have happened had 300 tons of ammunition exploded – it would have been total devastation. Driver Ernie Outram and Harry Grieve later towed the damaged 'K3' to Gorton Works with her motion removed. Harry described the engine involved in the recovery as a 'stretched Director', being none other than 'B19' No 1490 *Sir Sam Fay*.

Liverpool Central hosted several prisoner-of-war (POW) specials. Harry participated in a 17-coach train containing Italian POWs over the Woodhead route with driver Jack Coreless. Sensibly, a free-steaming 'K3', No 1332, had been allocated, giving him some comfort. The train was split at Central due to platform constraints, nine carriages being placed in Platform 1 and eight in Platform 2. After loading, the stock in Platform 2 was taken forward into the tunnel by the 'K3' and set back into Platform 1. I should add that the special consisted of new Gresley carriages with buckeye couplings, making it extremely heavy. The train, having been duly assembled, was standing in the middle of St Georges Tunnel near the old St James Street station, and due to the smoky atmosphere they were anxious to be away. Once clear, their 'K3' performed superbly, their wonderful run coming to a halt on Dinting Viaduct when a POW pulled the communication cord. Harry admits to being scared as he walked down the train only to find rifles trained on him, the guards thinking him a possible escapee. After steaming through Woodhead Tunnel they were relieved at Sheffield. He said that the tunnel was obnoxious, living up to its evil reputation, and they had to lie on the cab floor just to get some decent air. Harry describes the 'K3s' as the locos that won the war, preferring one to a 'V2', even if they were rough-riding engines.

The late Tommy Brownbill, 8A Edge Hill

Tommy kept an extensive record of life as a fireman and driver while working for the Royal Engineers, the London Midland & Scottish Railway and finally British Railways. These records are very detailed and quite superb, and there is little doubt that he was a highly accomplished writer. His early life on the railway is of great interest, as it concerns his firing duties with the Royal Engineers during the fall of France in 1940.

It was very hot when their unit arrived at Rennes, Brittany, their initial base. They were immediately attacked, not by Germans but by horseflies. Tommy states that they were three times bigger than common houseflies, possessing a very nasty bite. This created problems, as the men could not remove their battledress for fear of being bitten, and suffered greatly from the heat. Tommy did, however, find time to visit the city of Rennes, which he describes as being very beautiful. A soldier serving in the RE earned 200 French francs a week, whereas French soldiers were paid just 42. As you can imagine, it did not make for good relations with their French allies.

On 16 June they were instructed to marshal a train together for transit. This consisted of 75 ferry vans, the leading vans being NCOs' Mess, Cookhouse, Fitting Shop and Sappers' Mess. Their sleeping quarters consisting of four bunks on each side of the van, the entire train being pulled by an old 'Dean

Goods'. After a considerable struggle, they drew onto the main line at Bruz, where for some reason they threw a piano onto the train. Throughout the night and into the following day they slowly travelled down the main line, picking up refugees making for the coast. Eventually they picked up a priest who happily played the piano, keeping up morale. The locomotive fire had become very dirty by this time, so they had no alternative but to clean the ashpan and smokebox on the main line – not an easy job when you are extremely tired, sweaty, dirty and wearing full battledress; the promised cotton overalls had never materialised. After stopping at Sevenay, Brittany, they proceeded to Nantes, where they received orders to abandon their train. Everything had to be destroyed, including the engine. An enormous fire was lit before shutting off the water supply to the boiler. This led to the melting of the fusible plugs, collapsing the firebox, and leaving their old 'Dean Goods' completely inoperable.

As they made their way to St Nazaire, Tommy witnessed chaotic scenes as equipment was systematically smashed or blown up to keep it from the Germans. While under attack they found a small French boat that transported them to the destroyer HMS *Beagle*. On board survivors from the *Lancastria* told him some harrowing tales, their ship having been sunk the previous day with a terrible loss of life. Finally, much to their relief, they reached Devonport, receiving the freedom of the town.

Tommy had an eventful life in the Royal Engineers, until his discharge in 1946. I should add that I have only touched on certain details of his service in France, his journals being much more informative. I am sure that it was when with the RE that he met his wife Clarette, and it was at her insistence that he recorded his wartime exploits, together with his subsequent career with British Railways. I should add that Tommy was never a member of the Garston Coffin Dodgers, but his fascinating story at the beginning of the war deserves to be told.

The late Peter Lang, 8C Speke

Peter discussed his passed fireman's examination, stating that you went through the following procedures to see if you were capable of handling a steam engine. In July 1966 he was told to report to Warrington Bank Quay station at 9.00am, where a traction inspector would be waiting. Peter was questioned on trimmings and how they were used. Next he had to explain the valve positions around the wheel. The inspector then wanted to know what would he do in certain situations, and finally he was examined on the Rule Book. It was a very long and busy day. At 9.00am the following morning he was back at Bank Quay with the inspector, waiting for an express to Llandudno. Fortuitously, a 'Black Five' appeared carrying express lights, and the driver was asked to travel 'on the cushions' while Peter took his place in the driving seat. He now had the road, driving confidently and competently with the inspector silently watching his every move. Soon they were rolling into Chester, where they left the train to have a cup of tea.

Tea break over, it was off to pick up a 9F, standing with a train of vans. Again under supervision, he drove the freight back to Warrington, stopping in the siding opposite the Thames Board Mills. Soon the inspector uttered the magic words, 'You'll do,' and that was that. He never did get a piece of paper to say he was a passed fireman until he was made redundant in 1968. Peter had no time for diesels, and became the last passed engineman at Speke shed. In later life he became a driver on the Great Central Railway heritage line, having retained his love of steam.

John Anthony, 8G Sutton Oak

There can't be many men alive today who have fired Beyer Garratts, but John Anthony is such a man. When at Saltley in Birmingham he was often sent to Washford Heath to relieve Toton crews, occasionally finding a Garratt in charge of the train. These were one of the biggest steam engines ever to run in Britain, pulling 100 empty coal wagons with ease. After relieving the Toton men they took the Garratt to Water Orton for preparation. John states that they had a very wide firebox, containing a square drop grate, very useful when removing clinker. Some of the class had a revolving bunker, so that coal would automatically drop onto the footplate when required. Others had normal bunkers and were really hard work. For the fireman it must have been extremely laborious keeping up a sufficient head of steam. Basically they were two engines in one, and John describes working on them as memorable.

Later in his railway career he was transferred to Skipton shed, and soon volunteered to drive the various classes of preserved steam locomotives over the Settle to Carlisle line, including *Clan Line*, *Sir Nigel Gresley*, *Duchess of Sutherland*, *Duke of Gloucester* and numerous others. In fact, he sometimes comes to the club with his photograph album showing him at the controls of various classes. Jubilee No 45596 *Bahamas* was a great favourite, although for some reason he never liked driving 'K4' *The Great Marquess*.

Today steam locomotives are well maintained, which was sadly not the case under British Railways, especially towards the end of steam. Perhaps his main claim to fame was driving *Mallard* on her penultimate journey before her incarceration in the National Railway Museum. John is simply another driver who loved steam, and happily retains many memories of his days on the footplate.

Bobby Ellis, 8C Speke

Like a lot of drivers, Bobby used to wonder why certain engines steamed well and others did not. They were all the same class, had the same grade of coal, and yet some would not steam. He'd look at the shed board to see his allocated loco, and immediately know what sort of day to expect. The BR Standard '9F's had a tendency to derail, but were acknowledged as being superior (provided they steamed) to the Stanier 8Fs. He also recalled that in the 1950s, Speke shed had a small allocation of

I ONCE ASKED AN OLD ENGINE

I once asked an old engine, 'How do you work?'
And received a sly wink, shrug and a smirk,
'Well', said the engine, looking quite proud,
'It's the steam that I utter that makes me so loud
Created by my boiler, it travels around
Through superheater elements before cylinder bound.
Once in my cylinders, it expands with great force
Pushing my pistons with the power of a horse
Then it escapes up the chimney drawing the fire
Pushing out smoke, like an old funeral pyre.'
'What turns your wheels?' I quickly cried out.
'Be patient lad, you haven't heard owt,
The pistons you see, are connected to rods
And these turn all driving wheels through coupling rods.'
'Plenty of rods!' I excitedly cried.
The old engine now tooted and quietly sighed.
'Will you let me continue there's a little bit more?'
'Sorry,' I muttered, feeling quite sore.
'Ah, what was i saying? Oh I remember, the wheels,
When it's icy and wet, they can be slippery eels
Then I need dry sand to help find my feet
Just as you use grit in the street.
'What does your fire do? You still haven't said.'
'Will you stop interrupting?' he steamed and went red.
'Oh yes, my fire, well it produces the heat
In a copper container that conducts it a treat.
You see water in my boiler is then turned to steam.
Watch any kettle lad, you'll see what I mean.
The steam in my boiler it then travels around
Through supeheater elements before cylinder bound.'
'You've already said that,'I quickly replied.
'Well we're back where we started, care for a ride?'
I rode the old engine all night till I woke
Funny the bedroom was not full of smoke!
Dreams can be real when imagination runs wild
And an old engine can talk through the mind of a child.

Barry Allen

former Lancashire & Yorkshire engines, tank and tender. The
tender locos were excellent for tripping, although their cabs,
or lack of them, left a lot to be desired. He recalled that they
were numbered 52232 and 52438, but could not be certain.
The saddle tank versions were engaged on shunting duties,
reputedly having poor brakes. Speke predominantly handled
freight, and the movement of coal to Garston Dock often
dominated their working day. Bobby, like many others, enjoyed
his time at the shed, and regularly attends the meetings at the
Swan public house.

Fred Goulding, 8B Dallam

At Dallam they had a young black engine tube cleaner on
night shift, who was nicknamed 'Bo Bo'. He normally finished
his duties around 3.00am, always managing to find a place to
sleep for the remainder of the shift. For some particular reason
he decided to sleep on a 'Black Five' and curled up under the
smokebox door. It was not long before he was sound asleep,
but the engine was due off shed early in the morning to work
the 6.00am train to Carlisle. Her driver, Cliff Taylor, came off
shed and slowly reversed the engine tender-first towards
Warrington Bank Quay station, a distance of approximately
a mile. 'Bo Bo' was still fast asleep while all this was going on
and did not wake up until the engine coupled up at Bank Quay.
The next thing the driver knew was 'Bo Bo' appearing in the
cab wanting to know where the hell he was. Luckily he never
fell off, or it would have proved to be a memorable and painful
experience. An amazing but true tale – it appears that some
people can really 'sleep on a clothes line', or a steam engine,
without any ill effects.

The late Ray Hesby, 8C Speke

Ray was always cheerful and a keen gardener. Now, I am not
saying that Speke men drove the Stanier 8Fs slowly, but Ray
could leap off the engine, run around a field collecting horse

manure and leap on again while the engine was gathering speed. Truly a remarkable man! He told me about a trip from Sheffield to Liverpool Lime Street with two Class 31 diesels, one of which immediately expired. Before he left Sheffield he asked if the dead diesel could be removed, as he had eight carriages and did not want to pull additional weight. Unfortunately this was not possible, so he started his journey towing the dead diesel. Now, the 31s were not particularly powerful, his speed being reduced to approximately 30mph. Ray knew that he was losing time, and the passengers, thinking two diesels were in front, were expected him to fly. By now Ray was getting worried, as he was holding up other rail traffic and being continually checked by signals. Well over 2½ late, he finally reached Lime Street. Ray's immediate reaction was to hide in the cab while the public vented their anger on any BR official in the vicinity. A few passengers banged on the cab windows out of sheer frustration, and he later emerged to book off. It had been one of those days!

A. C. Jones, 27F Brunswick

A 'J10' pulled into Hunts Cross station on the slow line, heading for Brunswick shed. After being held by signals, her driver said to the young fireman, 'I'm going for a quick pint – I'll only be a few minutes,' and off he went. As the minutes went by the fireman became increasingly anxious, continually looking at his watch and the signals. After an eternity the starter came off, indicating that the engine was clear to proceed. Still he had no driver and was becoming more and more agitated. Suddenly a porter arrived and asked why they had not gone forward. The lad replied that he was waiting for his driver; however, he was told to proceed as the engine was holding up traffic. The fireman, with only a few weeks' training, somehow managed to drive down the main line to Brunswick shed. After disposing the 'J10', he booked off, including his absent driver as he did so.

The next morning the shed master sent for him and asked what time the pair had booked off. The lad out of loyalty to his ver gave his reply, only to be informed that his driver was in spital with serious concussion, having fallen when leaving the b. I am sure that this tale is familiar to those who have been similar situations, and I have heard many stories to this effect. yalty is one thing, but it must not be taken advantage of, and I ar there were times when it was!

ddie Meade, 8D Widnes

low we come to a man mentioned earlier in the book, Widnes river Eddie Meade, one of life's characters. Unfortunately he is ot a member of the Garston Coffin Dodgers, but I have made im an honorary member. His stories are humorous in the xtreme, and I will finish with one of them.

Liverpool Lime Street used banking engines, known as inties', to push the main trains part way up the steep gradient o Edge Hill. This was custom and practice, having taken place or as long as I can remember. One day a couple of 'GIs' from he American base at Burtonwood sauntered up to the crew of the banking engine that was waiting to push a London train, pulled by a 'Royal Scot', up the incline.

'Hey buddy, are you the engineer?'

The driver looked at them in astonishment, before realising that he was. 'I'm the driver,' he replied.

'Well, just get us to London on time,' replied the soldiers, handing the driver two bottles of bourbon.

The driver, being a typical Scouser, immediately grabbed the bottles and placed them in the cab before giving the GIs a big smile. They left, quietly satisfied that they had done their level best to ensure a speedy ride to London. As for the banking crew, they duly obliged, giving the London a hefty shove out of Lime Street, and a good time was had by all!

Finally I will leave you with some of the nicknames given to drivers and firemen working for BR in the Merseyside area, as supplied by the Garston Coffin Dodgers: 'Brave Dave', 'The Blind Snowman', 'Waterbuck', 'The Seldom Seen Kid',

'Dancing Dick', 'Pedro', 'King Billy', 'Bottom Nut', 'The Whistle Blower', 'The Ferret', 'Prince Oil Can', 'Wacker', 'Panface', 'The Sick Lobster', 'Snogger', 'Paraffin Jack', 'Torchy', 'Grunt', 'Puffing Billy', 'Growler', 'The Commander', 'The Mumbling Overcoat', 'Long Hours Arthur', 'Billy Bloodnut', 'The Oily Goblin', 'Diesel Dan', 'The Bandanna Kid', 'The Ghost', 'Call Me Driver', 'The Astronaut', 'The Black Bat', 'Laurel and Hardy' … the list could go on and on.

Your Author with John Kimberley doing a bit of firing(!) at the Llangollen Railway in August 1988.

I will book off now as it's time to make a brew. Thankyou for reading my book. I hope you enjoyed it!

Happy shunting!